Mushroom Cultivation

A Practical Guide to Growing Mushrooms at Home

By: Barton Press

Copyright © 2021 by Barton Press

ALL RIGHTS RESERVED

No part of this book may be reproduced, stored in a retrieval system, or transmitted in any form or by any means, electronic, mechanical, photocopying, recording, scanning, or otherwise, without the prior written permission of the publisher.

Limit of Liability/Disclaimer of Warranty: the publisher and the author make no representations or warranties with respect to the accuracy or completeness of the contents of this work and specifically disclaim all warranties, including without limitation warranties of fitness for a particular purpose. No warranty may be created or extended by sales or promotional materials. The advice and strategies contained herein may not be suitable for every situation. This work is sold with the understanding that the publisher is not engaged in rendering medical, legal or other professional advice or services. If professional assistance is required, the services of a competent professional person should be sought. Neither the publisher nor the author shall be liable for damages arising herefrom. The fact that an individual, organization or website is referred to in this work as a citation and/or potential source of further information does not mean that the author or the publisher endorses the information the individuals, organization or website may provide or recommendations they/it may make. Further, readers should be aware that websites listed on this work may have changed or disappeared between when this work was written and when it is read.

Table of Contents

Chapter One: The Wide World of Mushrooms 1
    Mushroom Basics 1
    Collecting Mushrooms in the Wild 3
    Why Cultivate Mushrooms From Home 3
    Mushroom Uses 5

Chapter Two: The Science Behind Mushrooms and Their Growth 7
    Basic Mushroom Anatomy 7
    Types of Fungi 9
    Mushroom Life Cycle and Sex 11

Chapter Three: The Basics of Growing Mushrooms 13
    Doing It Yourself Versus Using a Kit 13
    Cultivating Mushrooms Yourself 15
    Importance of Sterile Technique 22

Chapter Four: Choosing a Place to Grow 34
    Where Should You Grow? 34

Chapter Five: Different Mushroom Cultivation Techniques 49
    Making Grain Spawn 49
    PF Tek 57
    Five-Gallon Bucket Method 63
    Log Grow Technique 69
    Bottle/Jar Grows 76

Monotub Grow Method 82
Mushroom Grow Bag 87
Outdoor Bed Using Straw Logs 95

Chapter Six: Advanced Techniques 103
Agar 103
Self-Healing Injection Port Lids 112
Liquid Culture 114
Spore Prints 119
Spore Syringes 123
Drying Fruits 126

Chapter Seven: Popular Mushrooms to Grow 131
Lion's Mane 131
Oyster Mushrooms 135
Enokitake 139
Reishi 143
Wine Cap 147
Black Poplar 150
Maitake 153
Shiitake 157
Luminescent Panellus 162

Chapter Eight: Troubleshooting Common Problems 164
Contaminations Ruining Grows 164
Substrate Isn't Colonizing 165
Small Yields 166
Colonized but Not Fruiting 167
Dealing With Contaminants 169

Chapter One: The Wide World of Mushrooms

Mushroom Basics

While everyone is familiar with mushrooms, few people realize how interesting, useful, and diverse these fungi are. Mushrooms are fruiting bodies that sprout from a hidden network of mycelium. They come in a wide variety of shapes, colors, and anatomy, far beyond the simple button mushrooms and shiitake the average person is familiar with. From the truly alien-looking stinkhorn to the Pokemon-looking giant puffball, the forms that mushrooms can take are far more unique than many realize.

There are currently over 10,000 known types of mushrooms and scientists believe this is only a small fraction of what's really out there. According to some experts, there are an estimated 50,000 to 100,000 species they have yet to identify. Of all these varieties of mushrooms, some are excellent food sources or carry medicinal properties, while others are psychoactive or can be highly toxic.

Even the largest living organism in the world is a fungus. Armillaria ostoyae, also known as the Humongous Fungus is an organism that covers almost 4 square miles (2,385 acres) in the Malheur National Forest in Oregon. This fungus grows by feeding on the forest's tree roots, and this has allowed it to grow to such an epic size. The actual above-ground mushrooms only make up a small portion of this fungus, with the majority of its weight (an estimated 35,000 tons!) consisting of its underground mycelial network.

In the natural world, mushrooms play a variety of roles. Some fungi help trees to extract minerals and water from the soil, and, in exchange, the trees provide the mushrooms with sugars and other carbohydrates. Some mushrooms help in the process of decomposition, devouring rotting grass, wood, or other organic matter. There are even mushrooms that are parasitic in nature, attacking tree roots or insects.

For humans, mushrooms can be used for more than just food and medicine. Due to some recent discoveries, mushrooms could even be used to help clean up our landfills. In 2011, scientists discovered that the Pestalotiopsis microspora mushroom was capable of subsisting solely on polyurethane. In other words, they discovered a mushroom that thrives by eating plastic, a trait that could be quite useful in our world of disposable straws and single-use plastic bottles.

Another unconventional use for these amazing fungi is to clean up radioactive waste after a nuclear spill. Based on some recent experiments, there are three potential types of fungi that scientists believe may be able to absorb high levels of energy in ionizing radiation. These mushrooms seem to grow better in the presence of radiation and can turn this waste into something that is biologically useful. While more study is needed, this is just one more incredibly interesting potential use for these amazing organisms!

Collecting Mushrooms in the Wild

Although our main focus is to cover the cultivation of mushrooms, another popular way to collect useful fungi is through foraging them from the wild. This is especially true for certain types of mushrooms that are difficult, if not impossible, to cultivate from home. This includes some incredibly popular edibles such as the chanterelle, porcini, hedgehog mushroom, morels, and truffles.

However, the average person is not advised to go out mushroom hunting, unless they're extremely knowledgeable about mycology and the local edible varieties of their area. This is because there are a wide variety of toxic fungi, many of which could look quite similar to the edible varieties if you're not familiar with the slight differences.

Another problem with collecting mushrooms in the wild is the potential for contaminants. While mushrooms make great food for humans, they also make great food for a wide variety of other critters. This includes animals, insects, and other types of fungi. It's not uncommon to bite into a wild mushroom and find that it's loaded with worms or has nibble marks from some other woodland creature. While this won't kill you, it does make it a tad bit less appetizing.

Finally, wild mushrooms tend to have highly variable yields. During one growing season, you may find an excellent patch of oyster mushrooms and think you've hit the jackpot. However, this patch may not return, or if it does, it maybe small or infested with pests. With home cultivation, you won't have this issue. Each flush, which is the harvesting period of a crop of mushrooms, will spring up fairly reliably and offer a steady source of food.

Why Cultivate Mushrooms From Home

If you're reading this, you're obviously interested in cultivating your own mushrooms from home, and I'm here to say, you've made an excellent choice! Growing your own mushrooms can be an incredibly fun and fulfilling process.

While you're likely to run into issues and make some mistakes at first, it's all a part of the learning process. But when you're finally harvesting the first flush of fresh oyster mushrooms or tasty shiitakes, I promise, it'll be worth any frustrations you may encounter.

One of the big advantages of home cultivation is the huge variety of mushrooms it gives you access to. While the standard grocery store may have four or five types of mushrooms available, there are dozens that can be relatively easily grown from home. From lion's mane and reishi, to the bio-luminescent Panellus stipticus. These mushrooms can offer a wide variety of properties that would be difficult to find elsewhere as well, from decorative species, to medicinal, edible, and psychoactive varieties. The possibilities are seemingly endless!

Growing your own fungi can also save you money. If you tend to eat a lot of mushrooms, the costs can add up. Especially if you're a fan of some of the rarer varieties that are usually only available from farmer's markets or high-end grocery stores. While the startup costs can seem a little high, most of the supplies you'll need to buy for home cultivation are reusable. Therefore, these supplies can provide flush after flush without the need to purchase them again.

It's even possible to make money by growing your own mushrooms. Many rare edible varieties are in high demand in restaurants and farmer's markets. If you get especially good at growing some of these harder to find varieties, you can offer to sell them to local chefs or set up a stand and offer your own freshly grown produce. While growing mushrooms is not likely to make you rich, it is possible to turn your hobby into a side hustle.

My favorite reason for cultivating my own mushrooms is that it's just an interesting and satisfying process. From inoculation and watching the mycelium colonize to birthing and harvesting the fruits, the whole process is incredibly rewarding. Not only do you get to enjoy the harvest, but you'll learn a ton about these amazing organisms in the process. Mushroom cultivation also requires very little upkeep. As long as you use proper sterile technique and create the right conditions, most of the time growing is spent waiting on the mycelium to colonize and for the fruits to grow.

Mushroom Uses

Of the wide variety of mushrooms that are available to grow from home, there are quite a few different uses for them. By far, the most common reason people cultivate their own mushrooms is for a source of food.

Much like having a vegetable garden, growing mushrooms can be a fun and exciting way to produce nutritious food from the comfort of home. Some of the more common edible mushrooms people cultivate from home include oyster, enokitake, lion's mane, wine caps, and maitake.

Another common reason to grow mushrooms is for their wide variety of medicinal properties. Mushrooms like the reishi can be used for many purposes. Some of the medicinal benefits of this powerful fungus include enhancing the immune system, improving sleep, reducing stress, and lowering high blood pressure. Lion's mane, wine caps, and maitake are also grown for their medicinal properties.

Some home growers even cultivate fungus for their psychoactive properties. The most common mushroom grown for this purpose is psilocybe cubensis. However, in most countries growing psilocybe mushrooms is illegal and could land you in jail. For this reason, growing psilocybe mushrooms is not recommended.

And finally, while not nearly as common, some people enjoy growing mushrooms simply for their decorative properties. This includes brightly colored mushrooms like the pink mycena, strange-looking species like golden coral mushroom, or even bioluminescent varieties such as Panellus stipticus.

Chapter Two: The Science Behind Mushrooms and Their Growth

Basic Mushroom Anatomy

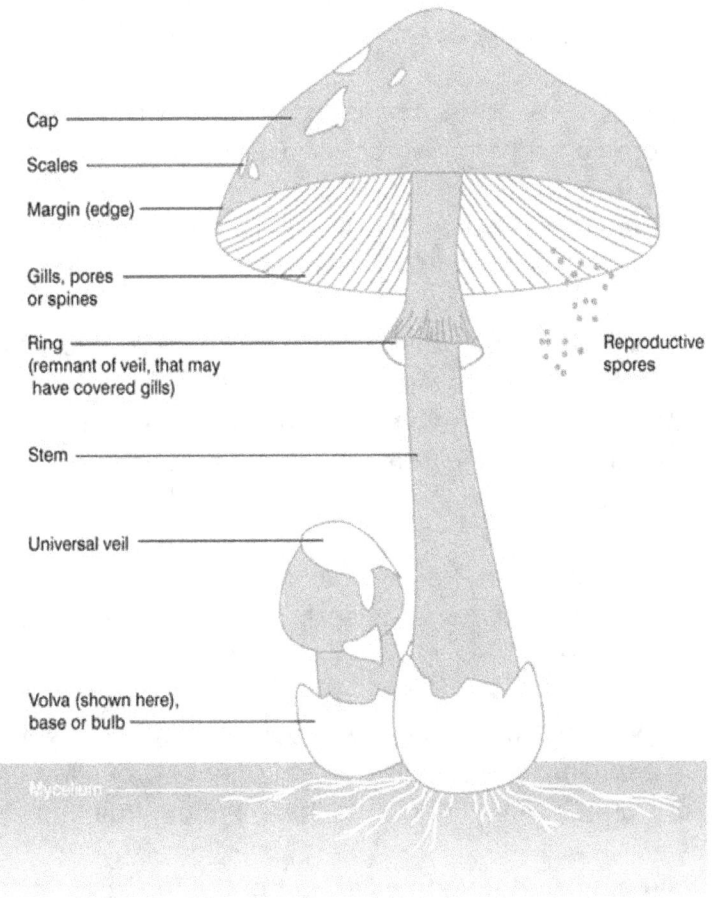

Mushroom anatomy can vary greatly, and not all varieties will have the same parts we list below. However, the average home cultivated mushroom will include:

- **Fruiting body:** This is the entirety of the mushroom which will emerge from the mycelium. Most fruiting bodies will consist of a cap, stipe, veil, volva, and gills.

- **Cap/Pileus:** The cap is essentially the 'top' of the mushroom. The gills are found underneath the cap.

- **Gills:** The gills, found under the cap, are where the spores are released once a mushroom reaches maturity.

- **Spores:** Found in the gills or pores of a mushroom, the spores are what mushrooms use to reproduce.

- **Stipe:** Often called the stem by most people, the stipe supports the cap of the mushroom.

- **Veil:** The mushroom veil protects the underside of the cap, where the spores are kept, until the mushroom reaches maturity. As the mushroom matures, the cap will flatten, breaking the veil from the stipe so the spores can be released.

- **Ring/Annulus:** The annulus is the small ring that remains on the stipe of some mushrooms and is a remnant of the broken veil.

- **Volva:** This is a cup-like structure that is found at the base of a mushroom. It makes up the remnants of a mushroom's universal veil that enclosed the immature fruit body.

- **Mycelium:** The vegetative part of the fungus that consists of thread-like structures called hyphae. The mycelium makes up most of the overall fungus and is usually found in the ground, or whatever substrate it is using as a food source, such as a rotting log.

- **Hyphae:** Small, branching filaments that come together to make up the mycelium.

Types of Fungi

All of the various known species of mushrooms can be put into three main categories, saprotrophic, mycorrhizal, and parasitic.

Saprotrophs: These are organisms that feed on decomposing matter (known as detritus). Other than mushrooms, saprotrophs also include mold and bacteria (common contaminants). Saprotrophic fungi release acids to break down dead tissue and non-living organic matter to be absorbed as a food source.

Of the different saprotrophs, fungi are the most efficient when it comes to decomposing complex organic molecules and recycling the nutrients back into the surrounding ecosystem. This is especially true for plant matter, which is composed of cellulose. They play a critical role in the carbon cycle and are incredibly important to the food chain. Without saprotrophic fungi, the forest ground would be littered with dead plant matter!

- **Common Saprotrophic Mushrooms:** Shiitake, Morels, Reishi, Turkey Tail, Maitake, White Button, Cremini, Giant Puffball, Enokitake, Chicken of the Woods, Oyster, Shaggy Mane, Yellow Houseplant Mushroom, and Black Trumpet

Mycorrhizae: This class of fungi has a fascinating symbiotic relationship with plants and trees. Mycorrhizal fungi play a vital role in soil biology, plant nutrition, and soil chemistry. There are two primary types of mycorrhizae: ectomycorrhiza and endomycorrhiza.

Ectomycorrhizal mycelium works with plants and trees by wrapping around their roots, Weaving itself into the actual cells of a plant's roots. Here, these mycelial networks will provide mineral nutrients, nitrogen, phosphorus, and moisture to their hosts. In return, the plants often provide the fungus with sugars like glucose and sucrose.

- **Common Mycorrhizal Mushrooms:** Matsutake, Truffles, Porcini, Chanterelles, and Caesar's Mushroom

Parasites: Not all of the relationships between plants and mushrooms are beneficial. Parasitic fungi survive by feeding on their plant hosts, which sometimes causes the death of the host. These fungi will usually enter a plant through an opening in the stoma, leaf, or lenticel.

There are also parasitic fungi that have a unique relationship with insects. Some of these fungi can enter an insect and feed on it without killing the host. Other parasitic fungi, such as the Cordyceps militaris, will invade a living insect and draw nutrients from it until it is able to fruit and release its spores from the unfortunate creature.

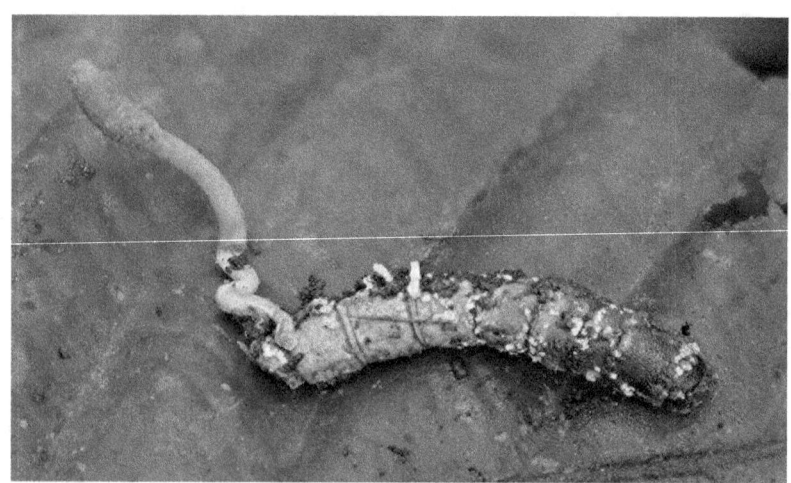

- **Common Parasitic Mushrooms:** Cordyceps Militaris, Honey Fungus, Caterpillar Fungus, Chaga, and Lion's Mane

Mushroom Life Cycle and Sex

Before you begin cultivating your own mushrooms, it's a good idea to familiarize yourself with how they reproduce and their basic life cycle. While this information is not entirely necessary for a home cultivator to know, being familiar with this process will give you an idea of what to expect when growing.

A mushroom's life begins with the germination of a spore on a suitable food source or substrate. This can vary from mushroom to mushroom; for some, it's wood or soil, and for certain parasitic species, it could even be an insect or a living tree. Once the spore germinates, the mycelium begins to grow throughout the substrate. This mycelium will release digestive enzymes to break down food and absorb the nutrients.

The mycelium will continue to grow until the conditions are right for fruiting. The aerial fruiting body, or mushroom, is essentially the sex organ of the mycelium and contains the spores which pass on its genetic material. Mushrooms are capable of both asexual and sexual reproduction. Sexual reproduction occurs when the hyphae of two genetically unique mycelia of the same species combine and grow together into one 'adult' mycelium.

The gamete of a mushroom is its spores. The spores are located within the pileus of the mushroom and are usually found underneath a cap. On most mushrooms, the underside of the cap is lined with gills that radiate symmetrically from the stipe. The gills are lined with basidia, each of which will contain four spores. These spores are composed of a cell and can survive incredibly harsh conditions.

A single mushroom can launch 31,000 ballistospores *per second*, adding up to an astonishing 2.7 billion spores per day! Each spore will have slightly different genetics, giving them a slight variation from the parent fungi. When growing mushrooms, variation can be minimized by cloning a mushroom that features desirable genetic traits.

Once released, spores will remain dormant until they come into contact with an appropriate substrate and the right climate and conditions are met. At this point, the whole process will start over and the spore will germinate to produce mycelium.

When mycelium is ready to fruit, it will produce 'hyphal knots,' known as primordia (among home growers, primordia are often referred to as 'pins' or 'pin sets'). The primordia will then differentiate at a cellular level to grow into the familiar mushroom structure (cap, stipe, gills, etc.).

The number of cells found in the primordia is exactly the same as the number of cells found in the mature mushroom. These cells grow by absorbing water and expanding to their full size. This very rapid process is the reason that mushrooms seem to appear so quickly after a rain. Most mushrooms are composed of around 90% water.

When a mushroom expands, its cap will usually start out as rounded; the underside, contains the gills and spores, protected by a veil. As the cap expands, it will flatten, and the veil will pull away from the stipe. The veil will eventually break away from the stipe, allowing the spores to be released. The circle, or skirt, of the veil that remains on the stipe, is also referred to as the annulus.

Chapter Three: The Basics of Growing Mushrooms

Doing It Yourself Versus Using a Kit

There are two basic options when it comes to growing your own mushrooms: buying a kit, or buying all the supplies, and doing it yourself. Both methods have their advantages and disadvantages. The best method for you is largely dependent on what you hope to get out of the experience. Now, we'll cover each of these in a little more detail.

Using a Grow Kit

There are a wide variety of kits available for growing just about any mushroom that is possible to cultivate from home. These kits usually consist of some already inoculated or colonized substrate. All you need to do is to introduce the spawn to the correct fruiting conditions and it'll produce fruits.

There are quite a few advantages to buying these kits. First, they're a heck of a lot easier and cheaper than doing it yourself. Making your substrate, sterilizing it, inoculating, making a fruiting chamber, buying all the necessary supplies, and everything else that comes with doing it yourself can take time and money. However, once you know the process and have the supplies, subsequent grows will get easier when doing it alone.

The main drawback of this method is that these kits can usually only be used once. Additionally, the flushes you'll get with a kit won't compare to the flushes you'd get from using a reliable DIY mushroom growing technique. But if you're just interested in doing a quick and easy grow to see if home cultivation is something you're interested in, these kits are a great option.

Doing It Yourself

If you really want to familiarize yourself with the process of home mushroom cultivation, doing it yourself is the way to go. Growing your own mushrooms from scratch does have its downside, but in my experience, the benefits far outweigh any negatives.

The primary concerns involved with doing it yourself are a larger time commitment, more work, and the initial startup costs. From preparing a substrate, making a fruiting chamber, and making sure everything is sterile, you will have to dedicate a decent amount of time and work to dedicate to this hobby. Plus, since you can't expect to get it right the first time, you will have to deal with a lot of trial and error.

From contaminations to accidentally preparing a shoddy substrate, there are plenty of downfalls you could run into during this process. But, for me personally, this all adds up to a fun learning experience. Once you get your process down and consistently grow large yield after large yield, you'll feel like an accomplished amateur mycology expert. That, in itself, is its own reward.

The cost of doing growing mushrooms yourself is not substantial, but it'll likely be much higher than the cost of a kit. Things like your pressure cooker, jars, and fruiting chamber can all be used repeatedly for future grows. So, while it may seem expensive at first, after you buy most of your supplies, all you'll need to worry about purchasing again is more substrate, gloves, alcohol, and other single-use items.

Additionally, you will have much higher yields when doing it yourself than you will have with a kit as most kits provide a small yield. Depending on your technique and experience, each flush could potentially produce pounds of fungi. While kits will give you a taste of the mushrooms you intend to grow, doing it yourself could provide a feast of tasty fungus and enough left over to share with (or sell to) others.

Cultivating Mushrooms Yourself

To grow your own mushrooms, first, you're going to need to buy some basic supplies. These supplies aren't definite though. Depending on the process you intend to follow, and the types of mushrooms you'd like to grow, the items you need to buy could vary.

Items You May Need

Spores or a Culture: As we previously stated, mushrooms grow from spores. Therefore, spores are an essential part of mushroom cultivation. Your spores will generally come in the form of a spore syringe or a spore print. A syringe is easier to handle and inoculate with, while a print will give you far more uses. Whichever you decide to use is up to you and depends on how much work you want to create for yourself.

If you want the process to go faster, it's also possible to buy a ready-made mushroom culture or even colonized spawn. A culture is simply mushroom mycelium that's either suspended in a liquid or on an agar plate. You can use this culture to inoculate multiple substrates and bypass the waiting time it takes for spores to germinate.

Syringes: Unless you decide to go with agar, you should have a syringe to inoculate your substrate (this also depends on the method/type of mushrooms you're growing). The most common type of syringe used for mycology is a 10CC Luer Lock style syringe with a 1.5" 16-gauge needle.

If you buy ready-made syringes, they can easily be reused. You just need to sterilize them in-between uses either by using a pressure cooker (make certain that the syringes are heat resistant) or filling them with boiled water and allowing them to cool at room temperature (this method also provides sterilized water).

Agar: While not absolutely necessary for home cultivation, using agar to isolate your mycelium before inoculation will usually produce better results. We'll cover using agar in more depth later.

Petri Plates: These will be used for preparing your agar. Instead of petri plates, it's also possible to use jars, cups, or anything that can be covered and sterilized.

Pressure Cooker: When growing mushrooms, sterile technique is of the utmost importance (more on this later). While there are some methods to sterilize your substrates without a pressure cooker, such as using water and steam in a pot, they simply aren't that reliable. Using a pressure cooker will ensure that any mold or bacterial contaminants are properly destroyed and won't ruin your grow.

Mason Jars: When preparing most substrates for inoculation, such as grain, birdseed, wood chips, coir, or sawdust, you'll need a heat-resistant receptacle to sterilize or pasteurize them in. Mason jars are absolutely perfect for this. Depending on the process you're following, the type of jars may vary, but, either way, you'll need jars on hand for most grows.

Growth Substrate: The substrate you use will depend on the preferred food source of the mushrooms you intend to grow. Some of the more common substrates include grains, wood, seeds, dung, and compost.

Perlite: Mushrooms tend to thrive in a humid environment, and perlite is an excellent way to provide humidity. Simply by soaking some perlite in water and lining the bottom of your fruiting chamber with it, you can create a nice humid environment for your mycelium to fruit in. But, once again, this all depends on what and where you're growing, as perlite isn't necessary for some fruiting chambers or for outdoor grows.

Glove Box: Once again, a glove box is used to help keep your whole process as sterile as possible. This is because, on average, there are between 1,000 and 10,000 fungal spores in every cubic meter of air. Protecting your substrate from these potential contaminants is vital for a successful grow. While it is possible to sterilize a room to work in, this has rather mixed results as it doesn't protect your mushrooms from airborne contaminants.

Therefore, if you don't use a glove box, there's a decent chance all you'll end up growing is a bunch of nasty mold. Luckily, a glove box is simple to make with some basic, easy to find supplies. We'll cover the process of making your own in the next section.

Gloves: In addition to your glove box, you should wear some disposable gloves to help keep everything sterile. It's not required to use sterile gloves if you make sure to wipe the gloves down with 70% isopropanol alcohol or hand sanitizer before working with them, but sterile gloves will offer an extra layer of protection.

Rubbing Alcohol, Hand Sanitizer, Bleach, Lysol, etc: While inoculating, making prints, or handling anything that could get contaminated, you need supplies to keep everything as sterile as possible. This means using Lysol or bleach to clean out your glove box and alcohol or hand sanitizer to keep your gloved hands and any tools you may be using as clean as possible. While it's not necessary to use all these chemicals, it's a good idea to have some of them handy.

Bunsen Burner or Lighter: If you're inoculating your jars with a syringe, you'll want to get the tip of your syringe glowing red hot between the different inoculation points and jars. This, again, is to help reduce the chances of a contaminant finding its way into your jar by way of the tip of your syringe. The easiest way to do this is using a Bunsen burner, but a simple lighter can also get the job done.

Making a Bunsen burner is a pretty simple process, alternatively, they can be found for sale online or in a science supply shop for fairly cheap. To make one, simply use a baby food jar, make a hole in the lid, feed a wick through it, and add a fuel source such as alcohol.

Fruiting Chamber: While some grow methods don't require a fruiting chamber, there's a good chance you'll need one when growing a lot of popular strains indoors. We'll cover some of the different types of fruiting chambers and how to make them a little further on.

Making a Glove Box

There are a lot of different glove box possibilities that you can make from home with easy to find materials. They range from fairly complicated to incredibly simple. For the purposes of growing mushrooms, a simple glove box is more than enough. We'll cover the steps for constructing a glove box for home cultivation below:

Necessary Materials:

- Clear plastic storage bin with clear lid (at least 60 quarts)

Necessary Tools:

- Felt pen
- Rotary tool or razor knife

Step One: Buy a clear plastic storage bin (to hold approximately 60 quarts.) Make sure that it's completely clear and easy to see through (clear as a glass window, you're going to need to see what you're doing through the box). These can be found at Walmart, Target, Amazon, or many other retailers.

Step Two: Measure in about four inches from the left and right sides of the box, and, with a felt pen, outline the holes (about four inches in diameter) you will be using to allow your arms to have access to the box. Use a round plate, pipe or other perfectly round with the correct dimensions.

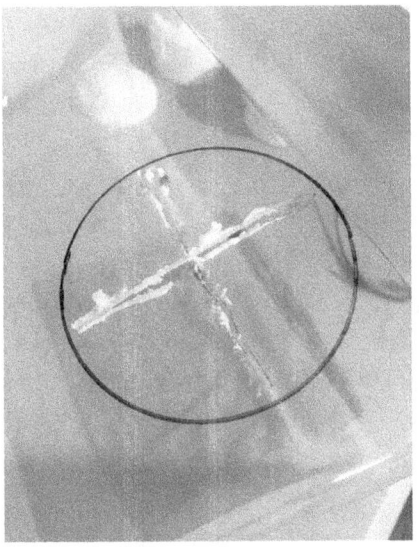

Step Three: Cut the holes along the lines you traced earlier. I used a simple razor knife for this, but be careful if you go this route. One slip could lead to a nasty cut, so go slowly. A rotary tool is more suited for this job, so if you have one handy, use it.

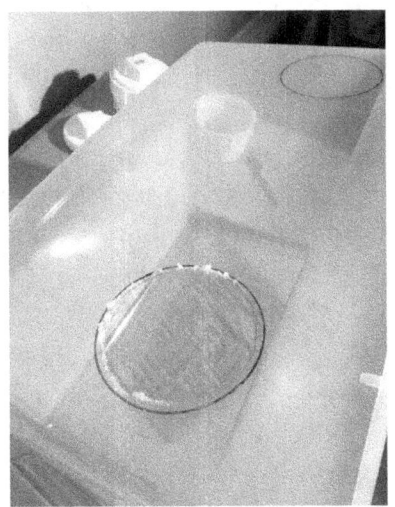

Step Four: In all reality, you can stop at step three and simply use your gloved hands through the openings in the box (that's how my glove box is). If you want to get more advanced, you can attach some four-inch PVC piping or toilet flanges to your holes and seal it off with some gloves. While this makes it look more "officially" like a glove box (the simple method is more of a still air box), the glove box is more difficult to work with and harder to sanitize between uses than the still air box.

Main Steps of Home Cultivation

The number of growing techniques is as varied as the types of mushrooms you can grow. From outdoor patches, to fruiting from logs, to using jars and rice flour, it's impossible to lay out the exact procedure you will use without knowing the types of mushrooms, substrates, and tek (technique) you intend to follow. With that in mind, I'll lay out the basic steps that are involved in most growing methods.

Step One — Choose a Mushroom: Everything from the substrate you use and the climate you need, to the process you follow will largely depend on the type of mushroom you intend to grow. So, first, pick a variety that sounds interesting to you, and read about the basic growing methods for your chosen strain. This includes the best growing location (indoor, outdoor, fruiting chamber type, etc.), which substrate/-s you can use, and how hard it'll be to cultivate. We'll cover some of the more popular strains later on as well.

Step Two — Pick a Substrate: Once again, the substrate you use will all depend on the mushroom you'll be growing. Some mushrooms thrive on wood, while others prefer grains. Sometimes a combination of dung and straw or flour and vermiculite is best. With some types of mushrooms, there are several substrate options you can choose from, all with varying techniques involved. So, once you've figured out the type of mushroom you'll be growing, figure out the substrate that best suits you.

Step Three — Prepare Your Substrate: Different types of substrates will require different methods of preparation. But generally, placing your substrate into mason jars with a measured amount of water and pressure cooking the jars at 15 PSI until sterile is pretty standard. But with certain techniques, such as log grows, this isn't necessary.

Step Four — Inoculate Your Substrate: If you're inoculating using mason jars, place the jars into the cleaned glove box (wipe it down with Lysol or a bleach solution), and either inject spores directly into the substrate or put a colonized piece of agar into it. This process, once again, can vary depending on the growing technique you're following.

Step Five — Wait for Substrate to Colonize: Your choice of spores, agar, or liquid culture as well as the type of mushroom you plan to grow can play a role in how long the colonization process will take. During the incubation period, providing a room temperature to slightly warm environment is usually ideal.

Step Six — Birthing Your Spawn: Once your substrate is fully colonized it's known as spawn. At this point, you will either mix your spawn with another growing medium, such as coir, or go directly to fruiting. This all depends on the technique you're following. If fruiting, put your spawn in the appropriate fruiting environment.

Step Seven — Pinning: After anywhere from a few weeks to possibly months, depending on the type of mushrooms, environment, and grow technique used, you should start to see pins develop. This is one of the most exciting points in the growing process. Within a short amount of time after pin development, you'll be ready for harvest!

Step Eight — Harvesting: Once the mushrooms are mature, you'll be ready to harvest. To harvest your fruits, pinch the mushrooms at the base and slowly twist and pull them. Try to get as much of each mushroom up as possible without damaging the mycelium.

Once harvested, you can either store them in the fridge if you plan to use them relatively soon, or you can dry or freeze them for longer-term storage.

Importance of Sterile Technique

When you prepare the substrate, you're creating the ideal environment for mycelium to thrive in. The main problem here is that this moist, nutrient-dense environment is also perfect for growing all sorts of nasty bacteria, mold, or even other types of mushrooms.

These undesirable growths are contaminants and are exactly what you don't want to see. Growing a mold and having it sporulate in your growing environment will not only ruin your current grow, but make future grows difficult as well. A bacterial contamination is rather nasty and usually means game over for your current grow as well. Mushroom contaminations, while not as common, will have you tending to a mycelium that will grow an undesirable species from a spore that somehow made its way into your substrate.

For these reasons, developing an excellent sterile technique is vital for home mushroom cultivation. This means that the substrate should be pressure cooked at 15 PSI for 60 to 90 minutes (depending on substrate/density), the instruments properly cleaned, your hands sanitized, and a freshly scrubbed glove box used.

In the beginning, it's totally okay to go a little overboard when sterilizing, in fact, I recommend it. As you develop your technique and begin to better understand the process, you may develop shortcuts and alternative methods. This is totally fine as well, as long as the process you are following is producing nice clean spawn and beautiful fruits, do what works best for you.

Pasteurization

For some growing techniques, it may be necessary to pasteurize an additional growth medium to add to your spawn to produce larger flushes. A commonly used example is coconut coir. When doing this, pasteurization is better than sterilization of bulk growing medium.

An easy method of pasteurization involves:

Step One: Fill large mason jars with the growth medium and cover the jar with aluminum foil or a lid

Step Two: Heat a large pot of water to 160° to 180° Fahrenheit

Step Three: Allow the jars to sit upright in the heated water for around one hour

Step Four: Turn off the heat and allow the jars to cool at room temperature

Once pasteurized, pour the room temperature bulk growing medium (either directly in a fruiting chamber or in trays) over your spawn, cover either with aluminum foil or plastic, and let it colonize the additional food source. This should result in larger fruits and more substantial yields.

Common Contaminants

The three most common contaminants are mold/fungal, bacterial, or insects. Now, we'll go over the most common types of each and how to identify them.

Mold/Fungal

Fungal contaminations such as mold are very difficult to deal with and usually mean this grow is ruined. A fungal infection will often come in the form of discoloration or a fuzzy type of growth on your substrate or spawn.

Some of the most common fungal contaminants include:

Cobweb Mold:

This fast-growing mold has the appearance of white, fluffy cotton. Since it's very similar in color to mycelium, it can easily go unnoticed at first to the uninitiated. One way to tell it apart is that it will generally be a slightly different shade of white than your mycelium, usually a bit darker. But once it has totally covered the grow, the problem will be obvious.

Cobweb mold thrives in very humid environments with a lack of air circulation. If this becomes a recurring issue, try lowering the humidity and getting more fresh air into your fruiting chamber.

Pink Mold:

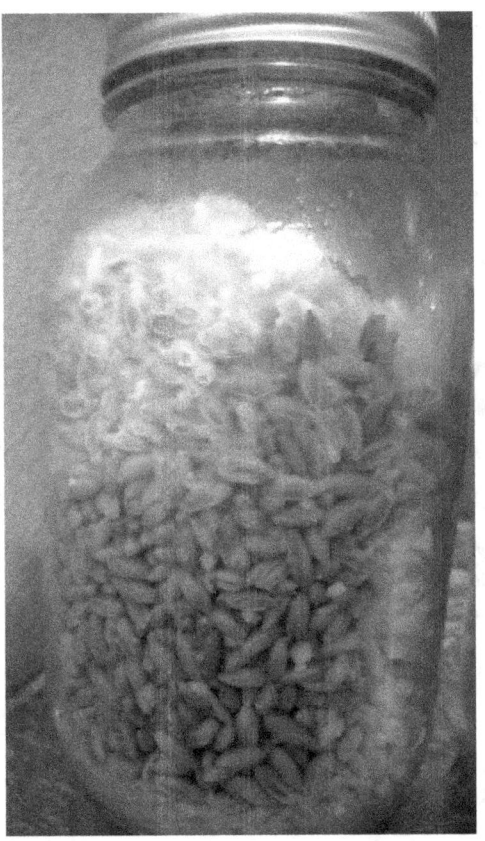

This brightly colored mold is also a fast grower and is most commonly found in agar and grain. Pink mold is virtually impossible to get rid of, so if you suspect it, throw away everything that's contaminated.

Green Mold:

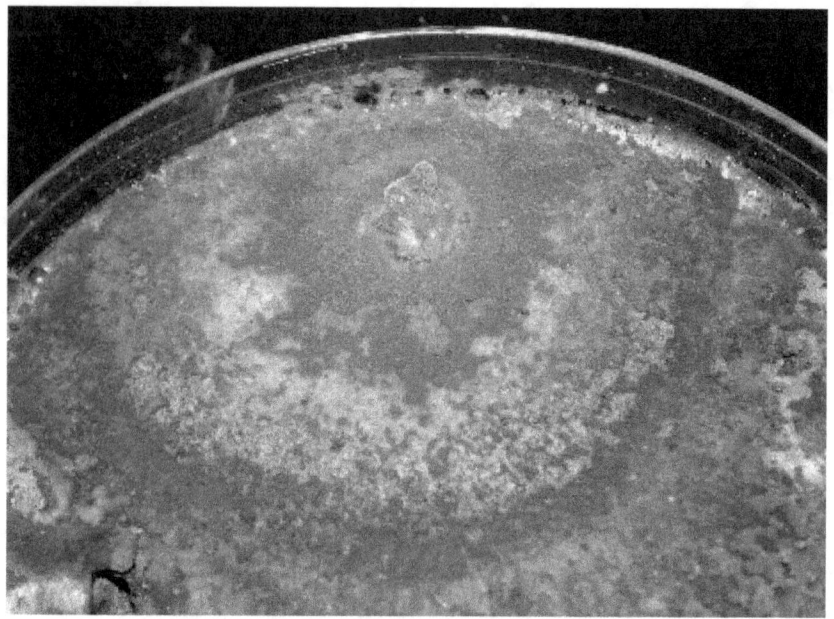

This species of Trichoderma begins as a quick-growing white mycelium that will aggressively spread across the grow area. As it spreads, it will cause soft rot and begin to release its spores. The spores it creates are an emerald green color, hence the name green mold.

This contaminant is especially common within the US and is the result of a dirty grow area and flies. Make sure to keep your grow area pest-free and clean it with a disinfectant, such as Lysol, to avoid green mold.

Black Mold:

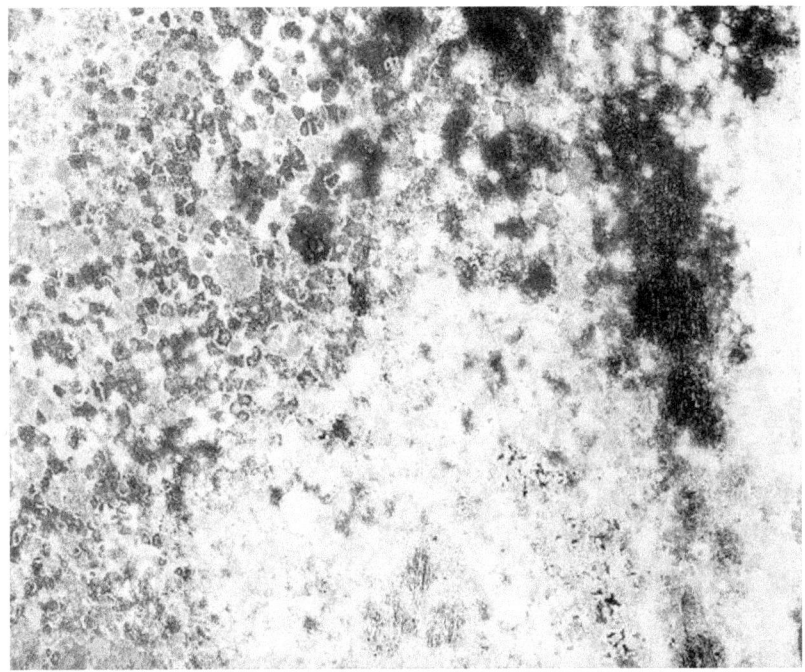

This mold can be found on just about any organic matter that would be used to cultivate mushrooms, but is especially prevalent on grain and agar. It can come in a variety of colors and is commonly known as Aspergillus. Aspergillus prefers substrates that have a neutral pH, or those that are slightly basic. Some species of black mold can be toxic, so if you suspect this contaminant, carefully discard anything it is growing on.

Dry Bubble:

Rather than a type of mold, a dry bubble is a disease that's caused by the Verticillium species of fungus. Throughout its growth, Verticillium goes through various stages that can be recognized. Early on, you can recognize this growth if your mycelium is producing pinheads that look deformed. As it develops, your mushrooms will grow with a tilted base and a cap that looks crooked.

Verticillium produces spores that are very sticky, so it can be spread through airborne dust particles. This contaminant also spreads through flies, so, as you should realize by this point, cleanliness is key to preventing this contaminant as well.

Blue-Green Mold:

Blue-green mold is an incredibly common type of mold that can form on the top of the substrate. These spores are airborne, which is one of the reasons using a glove box is so vital when exposing the substrate to the air.

Bacteria

Bacteria are single-celled organisms that quickly reproduce. The best way to avoid a bacterial infection is through proper sterilization and pasteurization. These infections aren't quite as damaging as mold could be, but they're still a huge nuisance for home cultivators.

They can usually be recognized by sight and smell. Many bacterial infections will give off the scent of stinky socks, far different than the nice mushroom-like scent of clean mycelium. A bacterial substrate may also look slimy, wet, give off brown or yellow stains, or have a crusty or gel-like appearance.

Some of the more common bacterial infections include:

Bacterial Blotch:

Bacteria blotch contamination will usually appear as strange, yellow lesions on or near the edges of the caps of your mushrooms. This bacteria spreads through the air using soil particles to catch a ride. They are more common if the fruiting area is overly moist, or humidity levels are too high. Keeping a fair amount of fresh air going through your fruiting chamber and lowering humidity should help you avoid this contaminant.

Wet Spot or Sour Rot:

Wet spot is an incredibly common contaminant as this bacterium is sometimes capable of surviving the sterilization process through its heat resistant endospores. This contamination both looks and smells awful. If you have a wet spot contamination, you will notice a light gray, slimy, wet looking area within the substrate that will give off a foul odor (similar to dirty socks). It will usually appear along the bottom of your substrate jar.

To avoid a wet spot contamination, soak the substrate for 24 hours prior to sterilization. This will give the bacillus endospores a chance to germinate. Once germinated, the sterilization process should adequately kill them off.

Pests

The final type of contaminants to cover are pests, which come in the form of insects that will feed on the mushrooms and mycelium. These contaminants are more of a gross nuisance and won't necessarily ruin the grow (as long as you don't mind eating the extra protein in the fungi).

Following are the two most common mushroom pests:

Mites:

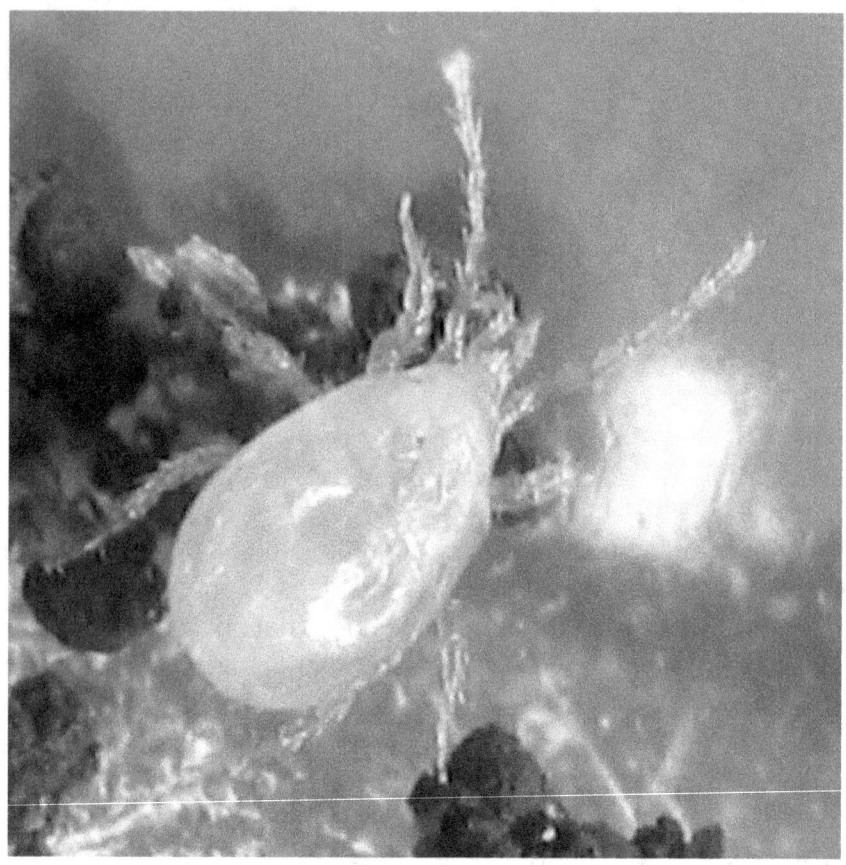

Many types of mites can be beneficial to mycelium as they feed on other types of common contaminants. They can also help to break down and mix an organic substrate, but not all are desirable.

There are some mites that will feed on the mycelium, damaging it and causing discoloration. Once again, keeping the grow area clean and sanitized is the best way to avoid them.

Fungus Gnats:

These small flying insects love the taste of fresh mushrooms and mycelium. They tunnel throughout the flesh of mushrooms leaving open spots that could be more prone to more severe contaminations, such as bacteria.

These gnats are fairly easy to identify, as they are tiny flying insects similar looking to a fruit fly. Keeping your grow area sanitized is also the best way to avoid these undesirable critters.

Chapter Four: Choosing a Place to Grow

Where Should You Grow?

One of the first things you'll need decide is where you're going to grow. Numerous factors should be considered including:

- The general climate and season of the area you live —
    - Do you live in a dry or humid environment?
    - Is it the right season for growing the types of mushrooms you want?
    - Is it hot or cold where you live?
    - How much rain do you get?
- The type of mushrooms you want to grow —
    - Will it be possible to grow these mushrooms outdoors where you live?
    - How controlled of an environment will you need?
    - What grow method is necessary for this species of mushroom?
    - What are the temperature and humidity requirements of this mushroom?
    - Can these mushrooms be grown indoors?
- The size of yield you want —
    - Do you want a giant outdoor patch?
    - Do you need pounds and pounds of fruits, or are you just interested in enough to get you through the week?
    - How will you store my excess mushrooms?
    - Do you plan to sell your mushrooms at a farmer's market or are they for personal use?
- The amount of space available for you to grow —
    - Do you have enough space in your home for growing?

- Will a fruiting chamber get in the way in your home?
- How much extra closet space is available to you?
- Would growing outdoors better suit your living situation?
- Whether or not you have an appropriate outdoor space for growing —
    - Do you live in an apartment or a house with a backyard?
    - Is your yard suitable for an outdoor mushroom patch?
- The growing method you prefer to use —
    - Can you use an indoor fruiting chamber for your chosen growing method?
    - Would growing outdoors be more suitable for this method?

Once these factors are considered, you should have a pretty clear idea as to whether or not an outdoor or indoor grow would best suit your needs. Next, we'll cover some of the basics of both an outdoor patch and an indoor grow.

Outdoor Grows

There are plenty of great reasons to choose to cultivate mushrooms outdoors. For one, some species of mushrooms tend to do much better in an oxygen-rich environment. Indoor grows tend to lead to CO_2 buildup, which could affect the appearance and yield of your crop. A couple of species of mushrooms that do better when grown outdoors include blue oyster mushrooms and king oyster mushrooms.

Another reason to grow outdoors is the yields you can produce. As previously stated, many mushrooms love oxygen, so the excess oxygen outdoors will give you bigger, healthier fruits. They may even be tastier due to a better environment. Also, depending on your home, you'll likely have more space to work with in your yard than you would in an indoor growing environment. This will allow you to make larger outdoor patches. Larger patches will lead to larger yields, which is ideal if you're a true mushroom lover or you intend to sell your harvest.

But outdoor grows are not all good; growing outdoors also has some negatives you need to consider. First, it's much harder to control the environment when growing outdoors. Depending on the climate where you live, as well as the season you're growing in, an outdoor grow may not be possible. For certain species, an unseasonable cold spell or a heatwave, could kill off your mycelium. Humidity is also a factor, and if it's really dry where you live, such as a desert environment, growing outdoors could be a problem.

Pests could also be a menace if you choose to grow outdoors. While you may love to eat mushrooms, you're not the only one. Everything from birds, rabbits, insects, worms, and other common outdoor creatures may also want to snack on your fungi. These things are much easier to avoid when your mushrooms are tucked away in your closet, but when growing outdoors, they can become a feast for whichever creature happens upon them.

The final possible issue when growing outdoors is the species of mushroom you'd like to cultivate. Some mushroom species are pretty particular, and an outdoor grow may be incredibly difficult. Indoors, everything from humidity to temperature can easily be controlled. Outdoors, you have no say about the weather or the temperature, so depending on what you're growing, an indoor grow may be a better option.

Now that we've got that out of the way, I'll cover how to make a simple outdoor bed for mushroom cultivation.

Preparing an Outdoor Grow

Below is the process of building a mushroom bed outdoors for growing wine cap mushrooms. These are by no means the only type of mushrooms you can grow using this process, and while you may need to use a different substrate, this technique could be used to grow a variety of species.

Step One — Choose a Location: To begin, you're going to want to find a place to set up your mushroom bed. Creating a raised bed that's lined with cardboard is ideal. Do this somewhere where the mushrooms won't be too exposed to the sun, like under a tree or a place where a shadow is cast throughout most of the day.

Step Two — Laying Wood Chips and Spawn: With this variety of mushrooms, you can use pretty much any type of wood chips, just make sure that they aren't treated with any sort of chemicals. Wood chips that are sold for smoking meats are a good option. Once you have your wood, lay down a single layer along the cardboard lining the bottom of your bed.

After the first layer of wood is laid, put in a layer of fully colonized mushroom spawn (see the section Making Grain Spawn in Chapter Five for the process of making your own spawn, or buy already colonized spawn online). On top of the spawn, place another layer of wood chips. Do this, layer after layer, similar to a lasagna, until your bed is filled. About 6.5 pounds of wine cap mushroom spawn should be enough for a bed of 13 square feet.

For the top layer, make sure that you use wood chips. Do not top your bed with spawn! Over the coming months, the mycelium will grow through the wood chips.

Step Three — Cover the Mushroom Bed: Now that you've used up your wood chips and spawn, you're going to want to cover it all up. A great medium to use for covering your bed is straw. This will help to prevent your mushroom bed from drying out, protect it from the elements, and act as insulation to keep it warm.

Once covered with straw, you should soak your bed with plenty of water. Your hose should be adequate for this. The moisture should keep it wet for a couple of weeks, but you'll want to keep watering your bed to make sure your mycelium has plenty of moisture to help it grow.

Letting your bed dry out could mean trouble for your mycelium, so for an extra layer of protection to keep the moisture in, a shade cloth can be used to cover it. If you chose a good shady spot to make your bed, this step isn't absolutely necessary, but it couldn't hurt either.

Step Four — Maintenance: If you live in a relatively dry environment, water the bed about once a week. If you get lots of rain where you live, this isn't necessary. Just make sure to keep an eye on it. If it looks like it's starting to dry, water it. Time and experience will help you determine the right time to wet the bed down.

After a few months, you can look under your straw to see how things are going. You should start to see mycelium covering the top layer of wood at this point. After around six months' time, your first pins should start to appear.

Step Five — Harvesting: Ideally, harvest your mushrooms before they get too big. Once the caps are fully open, they'll be more prone to pests and will begin to deteriorate rapidly.

Pick the mushrooms one at a time by gently gripping them along the base, then twist and pull at the same time. For optimal flavor, harvest them while they are relatively young. After the first flush, your bed should continue to produce a few more flushes until it is spent.

Step Six — Annual Feeding: If you'd like to keep producing mushrooms in the bed year after year, simply resupply it with a food source. This means adding fresh wood chips to it.

You don't need to add more spawn each year, as the mycelium should still be established in the existing bed. Just throw wood chips on the top, and use a rake to mix it with the existing mycelium. After this, just maintain and water the bed and it should produce more delicious fruits!

Indoor Grows

There are a number of advantages to choosing to cultivate your mushrooms indoors rather than building an outdoor mushroom patch. While the yields may be smaller, you have a lot more control over their environment making it perfect for any species that has very specific needs.

Growing indoors allows you to control vital mushroom cultivation factors such as temperature and humidity. Some mushrooms do better in cooler temperatures, while others thrive in hot, tropical, environments.

This makes outdoor patches dependent on the season and location. When growing indoors, these factors aren't nearly as important. With an indoor grow, it's possible to cultivate most species during the winter in upstate New York, or during the summer in the deserts of Nevada. As long as your home maintains an appropriate temperature and your fruiting area has the optimal humidity levels, your mushrooms will grow.

Another good reason to grow indoors is that it's far easier to avoid pests. Outdoors, your mushrooms will become a quick snack for whatever critters may happen upon them. While indoors, you still may experience things like gnats, mold, and bacteria, they'll be safe from the neighborhood birds and squirrels, not to mention many of the nastier creepy crawlies, such as worms and maggots.

Where to Grow in Your Home

When growing from home, you will need a space to fruit your mushrooms. Depending on the style of grow, you'll likely be using a large storage bin as a fruiting chamber. Since most fruiting chambers are pretty compact, there are plenty of great places to cultivate in.

Even in a small apartment (when I was in college, I was able to grow in a small studio apartment; it really doesn't take much space) you can likely find an ideal growing area. Just keep in mind that you don't want to choose a place that tends to get overly hot or too cold. This means that if your garage tends to freeze at night, or your attic is blazing hot during the summer, they may not be great options.

A couple of final considerations are air exposure and light. Unlike plants, mushrooms don't require light to grow. However, light does help to let a mushroom know which direction to grow in and to initiate pinning. Therefore, some light is a good idea. So, if growing in a dark space, a small LED, compact fluorescent, or even Christmas lights (the first two options are better) should suffice.

Also, small spaces that have poor ventilation can be used if you take some extra precautions. This is because in such a space, CO_2 buildup can hurt yields and lead to more problems with contaminants. To avoid this, make sure to fan the mushrooms frequently to dispel CO_2 and provide plenty of fresh air. A small fan can be used, or a fruiting chamber with a built-in fan is another option, but not necessary. When I grew in my closet, I used the lid of my fruiting chamber to regularly fan it a few times a day and that was enough to get the job done.

Some of the more ideal places to grow in a home or apartment of nearly any size include:

- Closet
- Cupboards
- Basement
- Garage
- Attic
- Grow tent

- Any other out of the way area you can squeeze your fruiting chamber into

Making a Fruiting Chamber

The strain you're growing, the method you're following, and the space can all affect which fruiting chamber would be the best option for you to use. With that in mind, I'll lay out how to construct several of the more common fruiting chambers home cultivators use.

Shotgun Fruiting Chamber

The shotgun fruiting chamber is ideal if you're following the PF Tek and a few other methods of growing (more on this later). It simply consists of a clear plastic storage bin with evenly spaced holes drilled into all six sides to allow fresh air exchange. You will also line the bottom of the chamber with perlite to provide humidity.

To create a shotgun fruiting chamber, follow these steps:

Necessary Materials:

- Clear plastic storage bin with a lid (size depends on needs, but most people opt for 60 quarts or larger)
- Coarse perlite used for gardening (10 to 12 quarts worth is good for a 70-quart bin)
- Large kitchen strainer
- Spray bottle for wetting down the sides of the bin
- If you want to get fancy, you can use a hygrometer for measuring humidity, but this is optional (if you use enough perlite, your humidity levels will be fine)

Necessary Tools:

- Power drill
- ¼" Drill bit
- Tape measure or ruler
- Felt pen

Step One: Buy a large plastic storage bin. Like your glove box bin, it should be completely clear to allow light to pass through it. The size all depends on how much mushroom you intend to grow. Your shotgun chamber can be tiny if you only want to grow a few jars worth of spawn, or huge, if looking to fruit a ton of cakes (cakes is a term home-cultivators use for mycelium covered substrate birthed from a mason jar).

Step Two: Now, you will measure where to drill your holes. This should be done on all six sides of your storage bin, including the lid and the bottom (don't worry about perlite falling through the holes, wet perlite tends to clump together so it shouldn't be an issue). Evenly space your holes around 2" apart in a grid-like fashion (think graphing paper) and mark each place you intend to drill with your felt pen.

Step Three: Next, drill the holes. Use a ¼" drill bit and a power drill for this. Gently press as you drill because pressing too hard could easily crack your storage bin. Make sure that there are no plastic bits left in the holes. Use a razor knife to scrape off any excess plastic that is left sticking out of the drill spots. Do this for every spot that you marked with the felt pen on all six sides of the bin.

Step Four: At this time, get the perlite and put it into a large kitchen strainer. Run tap water over it until it is fully soaked and the water is running clear from it. This will help to clean off all the small bits of perlite dust as well as moisten it before putting it into the fruiting chamber. Let the perlite drain after soaking it, but don't wait so long that it begins to dry. As an option, you can add a little hydrogen peroxide into the wet perlite to keep out bacteria and mold.

Step Five: Pour the wet perlite into the shotgun fruiting chamber. Ideally, you should have around 3" to 4" of perlite lining the bottom of the chamber. This doesn't need to be exact, but too little perlite and the fruiting chamber won't be humid enough. This is where a hygrometer comes in handy. If you use one, the chamber should retain around 80% to 90% humidity.

Step Six: Once complete, you can put the colonized cakes into the fruiting chamber. To help prevent contaminants, place a small piece of aluminum foil directly below the mycelium cakes so that they're not lying directly on the perlite (it should be just big enough to cover the bottom of each cake, you want plenty of exposed perlite to help provide humidity).

If the fruiting chamber looks dry, use a spray bottle to wet down the sides. If the humidity is right, you should see water droplets formed on all sides of the fruiting chamber. Regularly fan the chamber to provide fresh air and encourage fruiting. Place the fruiting chamber somewhere where it gets indirect sunlight, or provide an artificial light source, such as a compact fluorescent bulb. Time the light cycle for 12 hours on and 12 hours off to simulate natural light.

Monotub

Monotubs are one of the most popular fruiting chambers used by home mushroom cultivators. They also happen to be one of the easiest to construct. Monotubs consist of a large, clear plastic storage bin, with several large holes drilled along the four sides of the bin for fresh air exchange.

The bottom of the tub is generally filled with colonized substrate, which the fruits will grow from. As the substrate is moist, it also serves to provide humidity for the chamber. Monotubs will give you far more fruit than the average shotgun fruiting chamber, and are ideal for a number of different mushroom growing techniques.

The necessary steps to making a monotub include:

Necessary Materials:

- Large, clear plastic storage bin with lid (70 quarts or larger is ideal, size depends on your expected yield)
- Poly-fill or micropore tape to cover holes and protect from outside contaminants
- Optional duct-tape to help secure your poly-fill
- Optional plastic-safe black spray paint to darken lower half of tub

Necessary Tools:

- Something to make holes in your tub, a power drill with a hole-saw attachment is ideal, but a razor knife, scissors, or even gardening shears would work as well
- Felt pen
- Tape measure or ruler

Step One: Buy a large plastic storage bin that's at least 60 quarts. You can go larger if you want to have bigger yields. Keep in mind the space you intend to grow in so that you don't buy something that won't fit once it's complete. Again, your storage bin needs to be clear to allow light to easily pass through it.

Step Two [OPTIONAL]: It's a good idea to put something along the bottom of your storage bin to prevent light from coming through. Because mushrooms use light as an indication of the direction to grow, if you skip this step you will have mushrooms growing along the sides and bottom of your monotub (known as side pinning).

This can be done by applying thick plastic tape along the bottom half of your tub, covering every square inch, including the bottom, or by using a dark spray paint suitable for use on plastic. Alternatively, some growers just line the bottom of their monotubs with a black plastic trash bag, which can be removed and replaced with each grow. Using a trash bag makes it easier to take out your spent mycelium after harvesting a few flushes as well.

Step Three: Now mark the spots where you intend to make the holes. There are no strict rules as far as hole placement goes. As a general rule, make a 1.5" to 2" diameter hole that's just above substrate level placed every 8" on the long sides of the tub (usually two), and one hole of the same size on the short sides of the tub. The substrate level should be around 4.5" from the bottom of your tub.

You can use something round with a two-inch diameter to trace the areas you want to place your holes. A jar is perfect for this.

Step Four: Next, you want to make your holes. If you have a drill and a 2" saw-hole attachment, this is easy. Just drill out the holes in the places that you marked. If using a razor knife, scissors, gardening shears, or something else sharp, just make sure to go slow and be careful. One slip can lead to a nasty cut, so take your time!

Step Five: The final step is to cover each hole. You have two options for this, either micropore tape or poly-fill (the stuff sold in the craft sections for DIY stuffed animals and pillows). If using poly-fill, just stuff the hole until it's filled tightly with the cotton-like material. You can also use duct tape to secure it into place, but this isn't necessary. With micropore tape, cover the holes using just enough tape as necessary to do so securely.

This step serves two main functions. First, it helps to keep contaminants out of the fruiting chamber. But, since you'll be putting fully colonized spawn into the monotube, the mycelium will be mature, so contaminants aren't as much of a risk at this point.

The main goal of covering the holes is to keep the humidity in, while allowing fresh air to reach the mycelium. Humidity is essential for mushroom growth, as is fresh air, but if the holes are left uncovered, it will allow all the water vapor to escape and the humidity won't build to the ideal levels.

Plastic Grow Bag

These are by far the easiest grow chambers to make. They simply consist of a large, clear plastic bag with a ventilation hole in it, covered with a filter patch. These grow bags are also professionally manufactured and can be bought for fairly cheap online. Similar to monotubs, grow bag chambers are lined with spawn along the bottom, which provides humidity and allows the mushrooms to fruit.

To make a mushroom grow bag, take these steps:

Necessary Materials:

- Large, thick, clear plastic bag

- Filter patch that's 0.2 micron to 0.5 micron (easily found online)
- Duct tape or glue

Necessary Tools:

- Scissors for cutting a hole

Step One: Get a large, clear plastic bag to use as your grow bag. Ideally, the larger the better. Around 8" wide, 5" deep, and 18" tall is perfect. You also want a bag that's pretty thick. A flimsy trash bag isn't ideal (but not impossible to use), so a thick plastic bag is better if you can find it (look for 2.2 mil to 4.0 mil thick).

Step Two: Cut a hole in the bag that's large enough to allow fresh air exchange, but small enough so that your filter patch can fully cover it. The hole size will depend largely on the size of your bag and the filter patches you're using. Make sure to cut your hole along the top of the bag, a few inches down from the opening.

Step Three: Now, either glue or tape your filter patch so that the hole you made is completely covered with your filter. Make sure it is completely sealed around the edges, but that the hole in the filter isn't covered as you don't want to block it. This would prevent fresh air exchange.

Step Four: At this point, your bag is complete. You can use these bags to grow in, or you can fill them with substrate, inoculate them, and use them to make spawn for bulk growing methods.

When using them to grow, fill the bottom of the bag with fresh spawn and roll or tie up the top, allowing the bag to 'balloon' with air so it won't collapse. The filter will allow some air exchange, but likely not enough. Therefore, open the bag and fan into it a few times a day to provide additional air.

Chapter Five: Different Mushroom Cultivation Techniques

Making Grain Spawn

Regardless of the mushroom growing technique you decide to use, you will need some sort of mushroom spawn to inoculate the substrate. While it's possible to buy a wide variety of different spawns on the internet, you can also make your own with relatively little effort.

When making your own spawn, grain is the ideal food source for the mycelium of most mushroom species to feed on. There are a wide variety of grains you can choose from, including rye, wild bird seed, popcorn, brown rice, wheat berries, barley, millet, sorghum, popcorn, and even raw sunflower seeds, with the most popular being rye. Wild bird seed is also often used due to ease of access as it's widely available in stores.

Proper sterile technique is of the utmost importance when making the grains spawn. Your grains are highly prone to contamination prior to full colonization. Therefore, using some sort of disinfectant, such as Lysol, isopropyl alcohol, or a bleach solution, a glove box, and gloves are extremely important.

To inoculate your grains, you also have options. A liquid culture in a syringe is the ideal way to inoculate as it colonizes quickly, can be injected into the lid so you won't have to open your jar, and is easy to acquire through a variety of websites. However, colonized agar, another jar of spawn, or spores can also be used.

The steps making grain spawn are:

Necessary Materials:

- Grain such as rye, wild bird seed, wheat berries, millet, etc.
- Liquid culture syringe or spore syringe
- Quart mason jars with lids
- Poly-fill
- Gloves
- 70% isopropyl alcohol
- Bleach solution (10% bleach, 90% water), or Lysol
- Oven mitt

Necessary Tools:

- Power drill
- ¼" drill bit
- Glove box
- Pressure cooker
- Large cooking pot
- Bucket
- Strainer
- Bunsen burner or lighter
- Block of wood

Step One — Prepare the Grain:

To begin measure out the grains. Your sterilized jars should be about ¾ full. However, once the grains are cooked and have absorbed the field capacity of water, they'll expand quite a bit. Therefore, one full quart jar of dried grain should be adequate for about three quart-jars of spawn. It's a good idea to throw in a little extra just to be safe.

After measuring, rinse the grains thoroughly. This will remove any dust, crushed grain, and dead insects from the substrate. To do this, put the grains into a large strainer and put it under running water, regularly moving the grains around with your hand. When the water runs clear from the bottom of the strainer your grains are thoroughly washed.

Now, soak your grains in a five-gallon bucket or a large pot for around 12 to 24 hours. This step is necessary because some types of bacteria can survive the sterilization process unless they have already sprouted. Allowing the grains to soak will give these heat-resistant bacteria a chance to sprout so that they'll be killed during the cooking process. Soaking also allows the grains to begin absorbing some water.

Step Two — Prepare the Jar Lids

To prepare your lids, you'll need to create a hole that you will use to inoculate through using a syringe. The hole will also need to allow gas exchange and must be blocked with something to prevent contaminants from entering the jar.

There are several ways to create lids for inoculating grain spawn, or alternatively, you can buy professionally made ones through many mushroom cultivation websites. The easiest way to make them is with a drill and poly-fill.

First, set your lids on a block of wood you don't mind drilling into. An old piece of a 2x4 is perfect for this. Take a power drill with a ¼" drill bit and drill a hole through the center of each lid. Tightly stuff a wad of poly-fill through this hole. Stuff it in as tightly as possible to create an efficient filter from outside contaminants. Cut the excess poly-fill from the top and the bottom of the lid. When inoculating, you can do so through this filter.

Step Three — Cook the Grains:

Drain the grains after they have soaked for 12 to 24 hours and put them back in the strainer. The grains should have substantially expanded by this time after absorbing water. Rinse them once more and put them in a large cooking pot. Bring the water to a boil and cook the grains for about 10 to 15 minutes. If the grains begin to pop or crack open, remove them from the heat. You want the grains to stay intact as popped grains are more likely to develop a wet spot bacterial contamination.

Cooking the grains serves two purposes. First it will soften them which will make it easier for the mycelium to colonize and digest the grains. Secondly, it will allow them to absorb more water and reach full field capacity.

Step Four — Dry the Grains:

Once cooked, remove the pot from the heat and pour the grains through a strainer. To dry the grains, spread them evenly on a flat surface on a clean towel or something similar. Allow them to sit on this surface for a couple of hours to cool and to let the outer surface to dry. The grains are ready when there's no noticeable moisture visible on them.

To test if your grains are ready to begin sterilizing, pick up a handful of them. They should be fat and soft with water, but feel relatively dry on the outer surface. The grains shouldn't stick together but instead be separate, loose kernels.

Step Five — Fill the Jars With Grain

Load the prepared grains into your quart mason jars until they're about ⅔ to ¼ full. You need some open space along the top of the jar to allow you to shake the grains after sterilization, to shake during colonization, and to make breaking up the spawn easier once it's fully colonized.

Screw the modified lids you made in step two onto the jars once they are filled. It's a good idea to screw the lids on upside down (metal side down and rubber seal facing up) so they don't seal during the sterilization process. This will make opening them much easier later. Take a small square of aluminum foil and cover the top of each lid. The foil will prevent excess moisture from entering the jars during sterilization.

Step Six — Sterilize the Grain Jars

In this step you're going to use the pressure cooker to kill any contaminants living in the grains through sterilization. First, you need to place a rack on the bottom of the pressure cooker to prevent the jars from touching its bottom and cracking while they cook. Many pressure cookers will come with a canning rack made for this purpose, but if you don't have one, lining the bottom with the rings used for mason jar lids will work fine.

Pour about one to two inches of water into the pressure cooker and load the jars into it, placing them on the top of the rack. Seal the lid onto the pressure cooker and put it onto the stove at high heat. Once the cooker reaches 15 PSI, lower the heat so it maintains this level of pressure. Cook the jars at 15 PSI for 90 minutes. After 90 minutes, remove the pressure cooker from the heat.

Wait for the pressure in the cooker to return to normal levels. Once it's safe to open the pressure cooker, open it and, using an oven mitt, remove and vigorously shake each jar. This will prevent the grains from sticking together after cooking. Allow the jars to fully cool for around eight hours.

Step Seven — Inoculate the Grain

The first step of inoculating the grain is to prepare the glove box by sterilizing it. Using either Lysol or a 10% bleach solution, wipe the interior of the glove box thoroughly. Now, put gloves on your hands and rub them down with 70% isopropyl alcohol.

Take the grain jars and place them inside of the clean glove box. Wipe each jar down with an alcohol soaked paper towel to make sure they're as sterile as possible before loading them into the glove box. Wipe your hands down with alcohol one more time and take the syringe you're using to inoculate the jars. Using a Bunsen burner or lighter, heat the syringe needle until it's glowing hot to sterilize it. Use an alcohol soaked towel to quickly wipe off the needle and cool it.

Push the needle through the poly-fill filter and inject one to two CCs of liquid culture or spore solution into the jar. Shake it vigorously to mix the spores or liquid culture around the grains. Repeat this process for each jar, heating the needle between each one. Make sure to wipe your hands with alcohol frequently to ensure they're clean.

Step Eight — Wait for Colonization and Shaking

Take the jars out of your glove box and place them somewhere to colonize. An area that receives ambient light, is out of direct sunlight, and maintains room temperature is ideal. If you used liquid culture, you should see the first signs of mycelium spreading within a few days. With spores, it could take up to two weeks before they germinate, and the mycelium becomes visible.

Once the jars have reached about 30% colonization, shake each one vigorously to mix the colonized grains around the jar. This will greatly speed up the colonization process by mixing the colonized grains with the uncolonized areas allowing it to spread more rapidly. After shaking the jars, the grain should be fully colonized in about one week.

Step Nine — Using the Spawn:

At this point, the grain spawn is ready to use. This spawn can be used with most of the growing techniques outlined in this book (the only exception being PF Tek, straw logs, and a log grow). The spawn jars will have consolidated into a single mycelium block when fully colonized. To use the grain spawn, you're going to need to break this block up to make it easy to pour out and spread.

To do this, wrap the jar with a towel and hit it against something soft. I find that a carpeted floor or the arm to a couch works great for this. Just be extra careful not to hit it too hard as the jars will break if this is done too roughly. Once broken up, the spawn can be used to grow large quantities of mushrooms or to inoculate other jars.

PF Tek

The PF Tek, or PF technique, is a great way for beginners to start out when learning the basic process of mushroom cultivation. It's basically fool proof, and quite hard to mess up. While the technique was originally developed for the growing of psilocybe cubensis (the PF Psylocybe Fanaticus after all), the method can be adapted to grow most species.

The basic formula for this technique involves using brown rice flour mixed with vermiculite as a substrate. However, the brown rice flour can be switched out for sawdust, dung, or anything else you need depending on the requirements of the species you're cultivating. The PF Tek was originally created by Robert McPherson, the owner of Psylocybe Fanaticus, but has gained wide popularity due to its ease.

The steps to the PF Tek include:

Necessary Materials:

- Half pint wide-mouth mason jars
- Vermiculite (fine vermiculite is preferred but not necessary)
- Brown rice flour

- Syringe containing a liquid culture or spores (liquid culture is preferred)
- 60% to 70% isopropyl alcohol
- Glove box or still air box
- Gloves
- Micropore tape

Necessary Tools:

- Pressure cooker
- Power drill or hammer and nail (for making holes in the lid of the jars)
- Measuring cup
- Large mixing bowl
- Lighter or Bunsen burner

Fruiting Chamber:

- Shotgun fruiting chamber with perlite

Step One — Preparing Your Jar Lids: The first thing to do is to get the lids of the jars ready for inoculation. To do this, you simply need to create two to four holes, all on opposite sides of the lid, that are large enough to fit the needle of the syringe through. To do this, you can use a drill with a small bit, or simply use a hammer and nail to make the holes.

Step Two — Mixing Your Substrate: PF Tek traditionally uses a combination of brown rice flour and vermiculite as a substrate. However, if you're growing a species such as shiitake, sawdust could be used in place of flour (it all depends on the needs of the mushroom you're cultivating).

With brown rice flour and vermiculite, you want to add two parts vermiculite, one-part water, and one part brown rice flour. The amount of each all depends on the number of jars you're making. It's batter to make a little too much than not enough as these materials are all cheap. For six jars, you'll want about 4.2 cups (one liter) of vermiculite, 2.1 (half liter) cups of water, and 2.1 (half liter) cups of brown rice flour.

When mixing the substrate, you should always mix the vermiculite and water first, and add the brown rice flour after. Your substrate should be mixed well, and the final product should be nice and airy and not sticky. If you mix the brown rice flour and water first, you'll end up with a sticky substrate which is not ideal.

Step Three — Preparing Your Pressure Cooker: You want about 1.5" to 2" of water along the bottom of your pressure cooker. Make certain your pressure cooker can hold the number of jars you intend to sterilize. The jar lids should not be touching the bottom of the cooker or they may crack. Most pressure cookers will have a rack along the bottom for this, but if you don't have this, jar lids or a dish rag along the bottom will suffice.

Step Four — Filling Your Jars: Use a spoon to carefully fill each jar with the substrate. Leave about half an inch of air at the top of each jar. Make certain that there is no substrate stuck to the sides in the area with the half inch of air, and if there is, carefully wipe it off (any substrate stuck here will increase the likelihood of contamination).

Do not compact the substrate into the jars, as the mycelium will have an easier time colonizing the substrate if it is spooned in loosely with plenty of air. Once the jar is full, fill the remaining empty half inch of air with dry vermiculite. This will act as a shield from potential contaminants later.

Put the modified lids on the jar with the rubber side up (upside down) so they don't seal when pressure-cooked. Cover each lid with aluminum foil or thick paper to prevent water from getting into the holes you created when pressure cooking. Prepare as many jars as you can fit into the pressure cooker.

Step Five — Sterilizing Your Substrate: Place the jars into the pressure cooker and seal the lid, making sure it's locked into place. Place it onto a hot stove top and let the pressure cooker heat up until it has reached 15 PSI of pressure (depending on the level of heat from the stove and the size of the pressure cooker, this can take a while).

Once the right pressure is reached, reduce the heat and adjust it as often as necessary to maintain 15 PSI for one hour. After an hour, turn off the heat but DO NOT open the pressure cooker yet. Allow the pressure cooker to fully cool down for around 10 hours, and only open it when you're ready to inoculate the jars.

Step Six — Inoculation: This step is when the most care needs to be taken. Maintaining proper sterile technique during inoculation is key to the success of this process. This means that you should be using a still air or glove box, wearing gloves, sterilizing the syringe between injection points, and using rubbing alcohol to regularly wipe everything down. Over time, you'll refine your technique as you figure out what works for you, but the first time, going overkill with sterilization is ideal.

The first thing you should do is to wipe down the inside of the glove box with either alcohol, a bleach solution (one part bleach and nine parts water), or Lysol. Then get all of the materials you're going to need and place them within quick reach of the glove box, including the pressure cooker with the jars, a lighter and Bunsen burner, and the spore/liquid culture syringe.

Next, put on your gloves and use alcohol or hand sanitizer to wipe them down as well. If you're using a Bunsen burner, you can light that now as well, or, keep a lighter somewhere that's easy to access. Also, keep the alcohol/hand sanitizer nearby so you can wipe down your gloves regularly. Get a paper towel that's saturated in alcohol and have that in a handy location as well (but away from the open flame, remember, alcohol is very flammable!).

Now, you're going to open the pressure cooker and quickly load all of the jars into the glove box. Remove the foil or paper lid from the first jar. Wipe down your hands with alcohol, open the syringe, and heat the metal tip until it is glowing red. Once heated, wipe it down with the alcohol wipe and insert the syringe into the first inoculation point. Push down the plunger of the syringe until about 0.5cc of liquid culture or spore solution has entered the jar. Put the syringe into each inoculation point on the first jar and add about 0.5cc each time.

Once you're finished with the first jar, you're going to want to flame-sterilize the syringe and wipe it down with alcohol again before inoculating the second jar. Do this between each jar that you inoculate to prevent contaminations being carried from one jar to the next.

Always make sure the syringe is deep enough in the jar so that the liquid culture/spore solution is being squirted past the dry layer of vermiculite. To ensure this, put the needle against the glass of the jar so that you can see the solution drip down inside of it. This will also ensure that the mycelium will begin growing along the sides of the jar, allowing you to watch the progress and ensure there aren't contaminations.

Step Seven — Colonization: Once all the jars are colonized, you should place them somewhere and wait for the mycelium to colonize. For colonization, the required temperature depends on the species you're cultivating. For most species, room temperature should be fine. Place a piece of micropore tape over each inoculation point to protect it from contaminants while allowing for some fresh air exchange.

If you're growing a species that requires higher temperatures to colonize, an incubation chamber can be made using a reptile heating mat and a box. The top of the fridge is also a nice warm spot where heat-loving species can be colonized. Just remember, contaminations also like hotter temperatures and are more likely to develop if an incubation chamber is used. The heat may speed things up a bit, but they may also encourage mold and bacteria.

The amount of time required for full colonization will vary depending on the species you're growing and whether or not you used a liquid culture or spores. Expect full colonization in anywhere from a few weeks to several months. Once the jar appears to be fully white and colonized, wait about one more week to ensure the mycelium is fully consolidated throughout the substrate.

If discoloration, such as black or green spots appear or if wet and slimy spots form in the jars, they are likely contaminated. Any jars that form contaminations should be thrown away directly and not opened as this could spread the contamination throughout the grow area.

Step Eight — Preparing Your Fruiting Chamber: For PF Tek, you should use a shotgun fruiting chamber. To prepare it, fill the bottom of the chamber with wet perlite until it's about 3" to 4" high. Detailed instructions on constructing and using a shotgun fruiting chamber can be found at the end of chapter four.

Step Nine — Dunk and Roll: Once the fruiting chamber is ready for the colonized cakes, you can birth them and rehydrate them so they're ready for fruiting. To do this, first submerge the cakes in fresh water for 24 hours (known as dunking). The cakes will float, so place a plate or something heavy enough on top of them to keep them submerged (but do not squish them).

After 24 hours, take the cakes out and wash them under running water. Since the cakes are colonized, they are now resistant to most contaminants so you don't need to be nearly as careful at this point. Once rinsed, roll them in dry vermiculite or pour the vermiculite over them until they are evenly covered.

Step Ten — Fruiting: Now for the fun part, introducing the cakes to their fruiting chamber and waiting for pins. First, get a small square of aluminum foil to place each cake on top of, but make sure it's only big enough to separate the cake from the perlite and doesn't cover too much surface area. Place each cake into the fruiting chamber on top of a square of foil. Make sure the temperature and humidity in the chamber is adequate for the species you're cultivating.

Depending on the species, it could take weeks to well over a month before pins develop. Once you see the first pins, the mushrooms should mature relatively quickly. Harvest the fruits when they're ready and another flush should develop. On average, you can get around three to four flushes from each cake before they are "spent." It is possible to bury spent cakes in the garden or compost pile and potentially start growing fruits outdoors as well!

Five-Gallon Bucket Method

The five-gallon bucket method is a quick and simple technique you can use to grow a variety of types of mushrooms. Everything you need to take advantage of this technique can be found at your local hardware or big box store. On top of this, all the necessary supplies are incredibly cheap. While you can grow several different species in a five-gallon bucket, this method is especially ideal for oyster mushrooms.

This method is not only one of the easiest techniques you can use at home, but it's also capable of producing very large yields. The buckets will give you large sized fruits in good quantity and should provide several nice flushes.

The only downside is that this method is highly dependent on the climate in your area. This means that if you live in a desert or anywhere that's incredibly dry year-round, this technique isn't for you. In this case, an indoor grow is preferred (however, it is possible to fruit a bucket indoors in a controlled environment). It's also season dependent. Therefore, for the best results, spring, summer, and fall are ideal when fruiting the bucket outdoors (however, this also depends on your local climate and the species you're growing).

The steps to the five-gallon bucket method include:

Necessary Materials:

- Five-gallon bucket with a lid
- Wood chips (the ideal type depends on the species you're growing, but just about any hardwood wood chips will work)
- Large plastic tote bag (around 13 gallons in size)
- Mushroom spawn
- Spray bottle
- Large trash bag

Necessary Tools:

- Power drill
- ¼" Drill bit

Step One — Prepare Your Bucket: The first thing you'll need to do is get the bucket ready by drilling holes in it. These holes are where the fruits will spring out from once the bucket is fully colonized. The holes should be around ¼" so a ¼" drill bit is perfect for this step. Larger holes of around ½" to ¾" are also acceptable. However, the larger the hole, the quicker the substrate will dry out.

Drill the holes about two to three inches apart all around the bucket. You don't have to be exact here; just try to keep them a few inches apart as you go. If you'd like, you can also add some smaller holes to the bottom of the bucket (around ⅛") to allow excess water to drain, but this step isn't 100% necessary.

Step Two — Pasteurize Your Substrate: Now you're going to prepare the substrate by pasteurizing it. You'll likely be using wood chips or straw, but the substrate may vary depending on the species you're growing. Fully pasteurizing the substrate is an essential step for preventing contamination.

There are lots of different methods for pasteurization, but here, we'll cover one of the simpler ways to go about it. To do this, place all of the wood chips in a large plastic tote bag and fill it with hot water. The water should be between 150°F and 185°F to help kill off contaminants. If the tap water gets hot enough, that's fine. If you can't use the tap, a large pot or kettle can be utilized to achieve this temperature.

Let the wood chips soak for around 8 hours until they've fully cooled off. This will not only help to prevent contamination, but it will soften the substrate so that it can colonize easier later on.

Step Three — Get Wood Chips Ready for Inoculation: Once the substrate is completely cooled off, you can then drain the water. Make sure the wood chips are cool to the touch, as adding spawn to a hot substrate will kill the mycelium.

After soaking, the wood chips should be fully hydrated but they shouldn't be dripping wet as this will increase the likelihood they will get a bacterial contamination. If the substrate is over hydrated, squeeze out the excess water.

Step Four — Add Your Spawn: Next, you'll need to add the wood chips and mushroom spawn to the bucket. To do this, first add a layer of substrate that's about 1.5" thick. On top of the first layer of substrate, add a thin layer of mushroom spawn. Put another layer of wood chips on top of the spawn layer, and add another 1.5" layer of wood chips on top of this.

Continue layering the spawn and wood chips, one layer on top of the other, until the bucket is full. The top layer should be substrate and not spawn, so layer accordingly. You don't need to add nearly as much spawn as you do wood chips, as the mycelium from the spawn will colonize the substrate over time.

Generally, you can add about 90% to 95% substrate and 5% to 10% spawn. Using more spawn will help the bucket to colonize faster, but it's not necessary if you're trying to be frugal with the spawn. One five -gallon bucket will take about two and a half to five pounds of substrate.

Step Five — Wait for Colonization: Put the lid on the bucket after you've filled it with alternating layers of substrate and spawn. Now it's time to wait for it to colonize. While the bucket is colonizing, you should place it in a cool, dark space.

Ideally, you could store the bucket in a cool garage or basement. However, if you live in an apartment or just don't have access to a basement or garage, a closet or any cool place will work. The space doesn't necessarily have to be dark 24 hours a day, but it should be out of direct sunlight.

During this step, it's important that you don't let the colonizing substrate dry out. To avoid it drying too much, you can loosely drape some plastic over the bucket. Just don't wrap it in an airtight seal, as it's important that there is some fresh air exchange available so the mycelium can breathe.

After about a week, you can open the bucket to check the progress of the colonization. Just dig into the top layer of wood chips and see how the mycelial growth is coming along. The bucket should give off a pleasant mushrooms scent, so if it smells bad or similar to stinky socks, it's likely contaminated. It may also be contaminated if you don't see any growth at this point. If you suspect the bucket has a contamination, you should toss it, sanitize the area, and start again.

If there is a contamination, there could be a number of reasons for it. Most likely, the substrate wasn't properly pasteurized. However, it could also be due to contaminated spawn, a dirty grow area, temperature, or poor environmental conditions.

The time it will take for the mycelium to fully colonize is dependent on a number of factors, including the species and temperature. However, on average, the bucket should be fully colonized in around 10 to 21 days.

Step Six — Fruiting: After the bucket has fully colonized, you can place it somewhere to initiate fruiting. You should put it in an area where it regularly receives light. Ideally, light conditions should simulate natural light, with 12 hours on and 12 hours off.

If you live somewhere with an appropriate climate, you can place the bucket outdoors for fruiting. When fruiting outdoors, put it somewhere in the shade, out of direct sunlight, and in a place that doesn't receive too much wind to avoid it from drying out. If you decide to fruit indoors, you can use a compact fluorescent bulb to simulate a natural light cycle or grow somewhere where you get natural light from a window.

You should start seeing the first pins form within a week or so, but this could vary depending on species and conditions. The pins will start popping up in small clusters around the holes you drilled in the bucket.

Make sure the pins don't dry out, as this will cause them to abort. If the area you're fruiting in is too windy, loosely drape plastic around the bucket to protect the pins. Again, drape the plastic loosely so the mushrooms can breathe. It can be helpful to wet down the mushrooms a few times a day using a simple spray bottle.

Once the pins have formed, the mushrooms will grow fast. Expect pins to blow up into full-sized fruits in around a week to 10 days.

Step Seven — Harvest Your Fruits: Once the mushrooms are fully formed and the caps have expanded, it's time to harvest the fruits (if you're growing lion's mane, you'll have different markers for harvesting time). You should try to harvest before the mushrooms drop their spores, so do it before the caps have fully expanded and have begun to curl up.

As a general rule, harvesting the mushrooms too early is better than harvesting them too late. Mushrooms that have been harvested too late could start to lose their texture and taste different. Younger mushrooms tend to be firmer and have a better overall flavor, however, this also depends on the species you're growing. Harvesting early enough is especially crucial when growing outdoors as this minimizes the chances of insects or other pests feeding on the fruits.

Pull the mushrooms off in clumps, trying to get them off as close to the base as possible. You can do this by grabbing a clump of fruits at the base and slowly twisting them off, or by cutting them at the base using a sharp blade.

You can store the fruits in the fridge for the short term. For long-term storage, freezing them or drying them is ideal.

Log Grow Technique

Growing mushrooms on logs is a bit more advanced than a lot of other methods, but it has plenty of advantages. First of all, it will replicate the natural way that many saprophytic mushrooms grow in the wild. Species such as reishi, shiitake, lion's mane, oyster, maitake, and many others naturally grow on decaying logs in the wild. By growing on logs yourself, you'll be giving the mycelium optimum conditions to flourish in.

Using logs also creates a one stop shop for growing. The fruiting chamber and substrate will all essentially be the log. All you'll need to add to it is spawn plugs to get the mycelium started. Additionally, if you live in a wooded area, you can likely source the logs for free from nature.

Most mushrooms species prefer hardwood logs, but the best type of wood will depend on what you're trying to grow. For shiitake mushrooms, red maple, sugar maple, and oak work best. If growing lion's mane, consider beech, poplar, elm, or maple. Reishi prefers plum and oak logs. Oyster mushrooms will thrive on beech and white birch. Other logs that are good for many species include alder, birch, maple, balsam, elm, aspen, and willow.

One drawback to growing mushrooms on logs is that it takes mycelium quite a while to colonize and fruit when using such a dense substrate. Depending on the species you're growing, you may have to wait up to one or two years before the first harvest. However, after the first fruits pop up, you should receive a flush each year for up to six or seven years.

When selecting the log, try to pick one that is healthy looking and isn't rotting. This will ensure that there is minimal competing fungi already consuming the wood and it will help to reduce the potential for contamination. Smaller logs will colonize and fruit quicker than logs that are larger, but just about any log size will work.

The ideal size for a log is between 3' to 4' with a 3" to 10" diameter. It's also possible to inoculate a tree stump if you happen to have any in the yard.

The steps to the log grow technique include:

Necessary Materials:

- Hardwood log, depending on the species you're growing, oak, birch, alder, beech, maple, willow, elm, poplar, aspen, and balsam work well
- Spawn plug (sawdust spawn can also be used but it's a bit more difficult to work with)
- Cheese wax

Necessary Tools:

- Power drill
- 5/16" drill bit
- Hammer
- Old pot, crockpot, or fryer

Step One — Source Your Log: First you'll need to locate an appropriate log for growing the species of mushrooms you intend to cultivate. Most hardwood logs will work though. You want a log that is fresh and isn't already rotting or covered with some other sort of mold or mycelium to minimize competition.

This generally means the log should be relatively fresh. A log that was cut down from a tree within the last month is ideal. The log should be around 3' to 4' long and about have a 3" to 10" diameter.

Take note of the type of wood you're using, its size, and the strain of mushrooms you're using to colonize it. This data will be useful for tracking which combinations worked best for future grows.

Step Two — Determine the Number of Holes to Drill: Before you start drilling, you'll want to figure out exactly how many holes will be necessary. Each hole you drill will be filled in with a spawn plug, so this will also help you figure out the number of plugs you'll need.

Generally, a 4" log will require about 30 to 50 holes to put the spawn plugs in. However, you can use this formula to figure out how many holes the log will need:

Number of holes = (Length of log in centimeters) x (Diameter of log in centimeters) / 60

Step Three — Drill Holes: When drilling the holes, you should use a 5/16" drill bit. They should be drilled about 6" apart down the length of the log. It's a good idea to leave the top and bottom 2" of the log free from holes. The holes should be about 1" deep so that they can fit the spawn plugs.

Once the first row of holes is drilled, you should start the next row about 2.5" apart. The next holes should be positioned in a staggered row. The staggered rows of holes should create a triangle or checkerboard type pattern when complete.

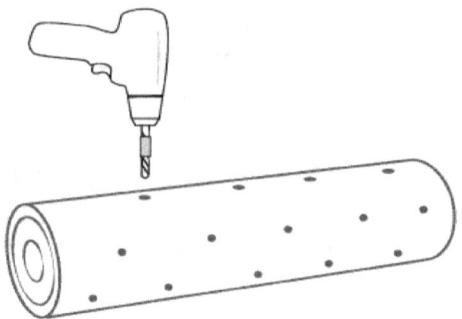

Step Four — Hammer In Spawn Plugs:
Now you're going to put the spawn plugs into the holes you drilled in the previous step. To do this, first push the plugs far enough into each hole so that they stay in place. To get the plugs fully into each hole, lightly tap them with a hammer being careful not to smash or break them.

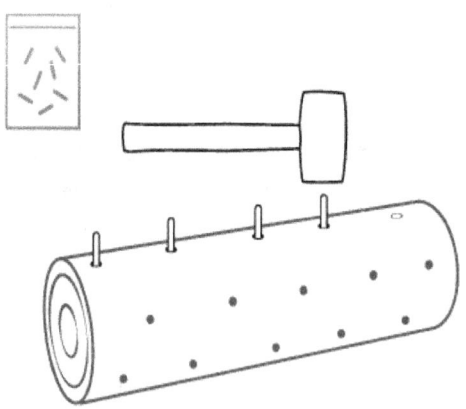

Make certain that the plugs are below the bark of the log, making them flush with the wood of the log. This will allow you to seal each of the holes to help protect the spawn. If you're using sawdust to inoculate the log, you should use a specialized inoculation tool for this step.

Step Five — Seal the Holes:

After each of the holes is filled with a spawn plug, seal them to help protect the spawn from outside contaminants as it colonizes the log. Wax is ideal for sealing the holes. Most home growers use cheese wax for this step, but candle wax and beeswax will also work.

To begin, first, melt the wax. You can use a pot and stove, a crockpot, or even a deep fryer. Just keep in mind that this will be a messy process and difficult to clean, so using an older appliance for the melting process is preferred.

Once melted, dip a wax dabber, brush, cloth, cotton balls, or an old cloth into the melted wax to apply it to each opening. Cover each hole with a thin layer of melted wax, making sure that it is completely sealed from the outside environment.

The seal is helpful in a few different ways. Primarily, it is used to prevent mold or other fungi spores from getting into the hole and colonizing the log before the mycelium has a chance to spread. It will also stop insects or other pests from eating the mycelium or making the plug holes their home. Finally, it will also help seal in the moisture so that the spawn doesn't dry out.

You can also seal the cut ends on both sides of the log to help it retain moisture. However, this step is optional and not entirely necessary for the grow to be successful.

Step Six — Store Inoculated Log

You will need to store the logs for quite a while during the incubation time. It's best to store them somewhere that's out of direct sunlight and stays shady. The side of the house, behind a bush, or under a tree will work fine. You could also use a garage or basement during this step, just make sure it's a place that doesn't get too hot. You can also cover the logs with a shade cloth to prevent too much sunlight.

There are several different ways you can choose to store the logs. One common way is to simply lean them up lengthwise against something, such as your house or a tree. You can also create a lean-to type structure, leaning multiple logs against one another so that the wait of one log supports another log.

If you've inoculated a lot of logs, it's possible to store them by creating a tower-like structure. This is done by laying two logs facing one direction and spaced apart by a couple of feet. Place two more logs on top of these but facing the opposite direction. Continue to stack the logs like this, alternating the direction they face with each layer. No matter how you store the logs, make sure they receive good air circulation and humidity.

Step Seven — Maintenance During Incubation:

If the logs dry out during the incubation period, the mycelium will die. To prevent them from completely drying, you'll need to hose down the logs about once or twice each week. Spray the logs with a hose for about 10 minutes each time you water them. This will ensure they retain the optimal moisture levels.

Another important thing to note is that the logs will need to be within the reach of a hose to make sure you can properly keep them moisturized.

Step Eight — Initiating Early Fruiting

While this step isn't necessary, it is useful if you're impatient and would like the logs to start fruiting a little early. By doing this step, you can get the logs to start producing fruits in as little as six months rather than waiting the two to three years it would take for them to fruit naturally.

To initiate early fruiting, you need to shock the mycelium of a nearly fully colonized log. Do not attempt this until around six to nine months after you've inoculated them. Shocking the log is done by allowing it to soak in cold water for 24 hours. This can be done in a cold stream or pond, a child's swimming pool, a bathtub, or even a canoe.

Step Nine — Harvest the Fruits

Once the log is fully colonized, it should start fruiting around one to three times per year. This will usually take place in the fall or spring and following a big rain. When the log is ready to fruit, check it frequently. Once pins form, the mushrooms can mature rather quickly, and you'll want to harvest them before they rot or are eaten by pests.

You should harvest the mushrooms when they're still fairly young and before they've fully matured. Mushrooms that are too mature will have a more fibrous and woody texture and lose the desired flavor.

If you're growing shiitake mushrooms, harvest them before the caps have opened and when they're about 2" in diameter. This is generally two to seven days after initial pinning.

With oyster mushrooms, you should harvest them while they still have a curl in their shape. Over time, the rim of oyster mushrooms will completely flatten, so just make sure you harvest before this happens.

Bottle/Jar Grows

Using wide mouthed bottles or mason jars to grow mushrooms is a fairly easy technique that's not too labor intensive. Growing in this fashion has plenty of advantages. First, unlike growing in bags, the materials can be reused, reducing the overall costs and the amount of garbage you produce.

Another perk to growing in bottles is that you will generally produce more uniform fruits. This makes harvesting easier and creates more aesthetically pleasing mushrooms that are easier to package and sell. However, there are a few drawbacks to growing from bottles as well.

One big disadvantage is that mushrooms grown this way tend to be smaller in size. Mushrooms that are given a larger environment to fruit from, such as a monotub, outdoor bed, or fruiting bag will grow larger and produce bigger flushes. Due to the small surface area, jar grows will only give you relatively few mushrooms that aren't very large.

Jar grows will also only produce a single flush. Due to the lower amount of substrate that you'll be using, the mycelium won't have a large enough food source to produce the multiple flushes that other techniques will provide. Even if a second flush does grow, it'll generally be so small that it's really not worth your time.

Not all mushroom species can be grown using the bottle technique. The species that will do the best when growing from a bottle include enoki, beech mushrooms, nameko, shiitake, and maitake. When using this method, quart sized mason jars work best.

The steps to a bottle grow include:

Necessary Materials:

- Quart sized mason jars with lids
- Substrate, the type depends on the species you're growing but generally you'll use either hardwood sawdust and bran or soy hulls
- Poly-fill
- Mushroom spawn

- Large plastic bowl
- Aluminum foil
- Gloves
- Isopropyl alcohol

Necessary Tools:

- Pressure cooker
- Power drill
- ¼" Drill bit
- Glove box

Fruiting Chamber:

- Shotgun fruiting chamber with perlite

Step One — Prepare the Lids

To begin, you'll need to prepare the lids of the jars so that they can allow fresh air exchange and stay safe from outside contaminants. To do this, you'll use a power drill and a ¼" drill bit to create a hole in the center of each lid.

Once you've created the hole, pull a wad of poly-fill through it so that it tightly fills the space. Cut off any excess poly-fill that's hanging from the top and the bottom of the lid, but leave enough to ensure that it stays firmly in place. This will act as a filter for contaminants while still allowing fresh air to enter the jar.

Step Two — Hydrate and Add the Substrate:

Now, you'll need to hydrate the substrate you've chosen for the type of mushroom you're growing. The substrate will usually be some type of hardwood sawdust mixed with bran and/or soy hulls.

First, place the substrate in a large plastic bowl or other container, and add water until it is thoroughly soaked. You don't want the substrate to be too wet though, as this increases the likelihood of a bacterial contamination. Slowly add water, and occasionally pick up a handful of the substrate and squeeze it. When it's wet enough but only a few drops of water can easily be squeezed out it should be good.

Next, you should fille each jar with the hydrated substrate. Don't pack the jars too tightly as this will make it more difficult for the mycelium to colonize. To pack the substrate, lightly tap it on a hard surface. Fill each jar until there is about a half an inch of empty space left at the top.

Step Three — Bore a Hole Into the Substrate:

In this step, you'll need to create a hole in the substrate that you will pour the colonized spawn into later on. To create the hole, use the handle of a wooden spoon or something similar and push it through the center of the spawn until it hits the bottom of the jar. You want the hole to be around ¾" in diameter but this doesn't need to be precise.

Once you've created the holes, handle the jars carefully. Moving them around too quickly or knocking them against something will easily cause the holes to collapse. Once you're done, seal the jars and cover them with a square of aluminum foil.

Step Four — Sterilize the Substrate

To kill off any mold spores or bacteria that could be present in the substrate, you need to sterilize each of the jars. To do this, first put a rack or a dish towel along the bottom of the pressure cooker so the jars aren't in direct contact with the metal. This will prevent them from cracking due to the heat during the sterilization process. Then, put about an inch of water along the bottom of the cooker.

Now, place each jar into the pressure cooker, making sure that they're all standing upright. Place the pressure cooker onto the stove and turn on high heat until it reaches 15 PSI. Once it's at 15 PSI, reduce the heat so that it stays at this level of pressure. This may take a little practice at first, but over time, you'll find the ideal level.

Cook the jars in the pressure cooker for around 90 minutes at this level of pressure. After 90 minutes, turn off the heat and let the jars cool in the pressure cooker for about eight hours. Do not open the pressure cooker until it has fully cooled.

Step Five — Inoculate

After at least eight hours has passed, the jars should be fully cooled and ready to inoculate. Open the pressure cooker and make sure that the jars are cool to the touch to make certain that they're ready to receive the colonized spawn. If they're still too hot, this will kill the mycelium and ruin the grow.

For this step, you should use a still air or glove box. First, sterilize the glove box using alcohol or a bleach solution. Then, quickly move the jars from the pressure cooker into the glove box. Also, place the colonized grain spawn in the glove box.

For each substrate jar, quickly open it and pour the spawn into the hole you bored into the center of the substrate. Make sure to do this step quickly and replace the lid as fast as possible to limit the amount of time the open jar is exposed to the air to prevent contamination.

Step Six — Wait to Colonize

After you've inoculated all of the jars, take them out of the glove box and place them somewhere to colonize. This can be done at room temperature, just make sure the jars are out of direct sunlight and that the space isn't too hot. Colonization time can vary based on a number of factors, such as the species and room temperature. Generally, it should take around a month to fully colonize.

Step Seven — Fruiting

Once the jar is fully colonized, it's time to introduce the jar to fruiting conditions. First, open each jar and scratch the top layer of mycelium with a clean fork. This will help to initiate fruiting and create an even pin-set.

After you've scratched the top layer of mycelium, place the jars onto the perlite in the prepared shotgun fruiting chamber. Leave the lids on the jars when putting them into fruiting conditions. You should start to see pins forming within one week. The pins should expand into full-sized fruits after a few days.

Step Eight — Harvesting

You should harvest the fruits before they fully mature and begin dropping spores. To harvest, grab the mushrooms at the base and gently twist them from the mycelium. Alternatively, you can use a sharp knife or razor blade and cut them at the base.

If you plan to use the mushrooms within a week, you can store them in a paper bag within the fridge. Store them in a breathable container and not a plastic bag to prevent them from rotting. For long-term storage, either freeze or dry them.

Monotub Grow Method

A monotub is an excellent way to get big yields while only using a small indoor space. Using a 70-quart plastic storage bin, you can produce several large flushes of a wide variety of edible and medicinal mushroom species.

Monotubs can easily be stored in a closet, the corner of the room, in the basement, or the garage of your home when fruiting. Preparing a monotub for home cultivation is relatively easy when starting from colonized mushroom spawn.

When growing using a monotub, the lack of fresh air exchange could be problematic with certain species. Mushrooms such as oysters require quite a bit of fresh air, making a bucket or log grow more ideal. However, this doesn't mean it's impossible.

When growing a variety that requires plenty of fresh air, a small computer fan can be attached to the fruiting chamber to maximize airflow. Alternatively, if attaching a fan seems too labor-intensive, simply fanning the tub several times each day should suffice. This may result in smaller or deformed fruits, but they'll still taste great.

The steps to the monotub grow method include:

Necessary Materials:

- Mushrooms spawn
- Bulk substrate, this depends on the species you're growing, but coconut coir, sawdust, dung, and straw can all be used.
- Quart mason jars with lids.
- 70% isopropyl alcohol or bleach solution (10% bleach, 90% water).

Necessary Tools:

- Large pot
- Spray bottle

Fruiting Chamber:

- Monotub

Step One — Hydrate the Substrate:

The first thing you'll need to do is hydrate the bulk substrate. Regardless of the substrate you're using, you don't want to add too much water to it. If you over-hydrate the substrate, you greatly increase the risk of bacterial contamination.

To hydrate the substrate, keep adding water to it and regularly pick up a handful of the substrate and give it a good squeeze. When a few drops of water easily drip down after squeezing a handful of substrate, stop adding water.

Step Two — Pasteurize the Bulk Substrate

Now, fill the quart sized mason jars with the hydrated substrate. The number of jars you'll need will depend on the size of the monotub, but around 8 to ten quart-sized jars of substrate should suffice. Put the lids on the jars but don't tighten them too much as to avoid them from sealing and being difficult to open later on.

Place the jars in a large pot and fill it with water until it's just below the lids of the jars. Put the pot on a stove and heat the water until it reaches 160° to 180° Fahrenheit. Allow the jars to sit in the heated water for about one hour. After an hour has passed, remove the pot from the heat and allow the substrate jars to cool for six to eight hours.

Step Three — Sterilize Monotub

Before adding the substrate and spawn to the monotub, it should be sterilized to ensure it's free from contaminants such as mold spores and bacteria. To do this, start by putting either 70% isopropyl alcohol or a 10% bleach solution into a spray bottle.

Spray the solution on the inside of the monotub and wipe it off with a clean paper towel or rag. Now the fruiting chamber is ready so you can start adding the substrate and mushroom spawn.

Step Four — Layer Substrate and Spawn:

After the bulk substrate has returned to room temperature, you can remove it from the water. Make sure the jars are cool to the touch. If the bulk substrate is too hot, it will kill the colonized spawn and ruin the grow.

Open a jar of bulk substrate and sprinkle about one inch of it along the bottom of the monotub. Next, add about one half inch of mushroom spawn to the top of the substrate. On top of the spawn, add another inch of bulk substrate. Continue layering the substrate and spawn, similar to a lasagna, until it's about three to five inches thick.

Top it off with another one-inch layer of substrate. When you've reached the desired thickness, place the lid back on top of the monotub. Optionally, you can cover the spawn and substrate layers with a black trash bag to help keep in moisture during the colonization process.

Step Five — Wait for Colonization:

When the monotub is loaded with the substrate and spawn mix, place it somewhere to colonize. Someplace that is out of direct sunlight, but still receives some ambient light and is ideal. A warm environment can speed up colonization (but it should not be too hot, as this can kill the mycelium or lead to contamination), but room temperature is fine.

After a few days, check the top layer of substrate to see if there are any signs of colonization. Ideally, you should start seeing white spots of mycelium spreading across the top layer of substrate.

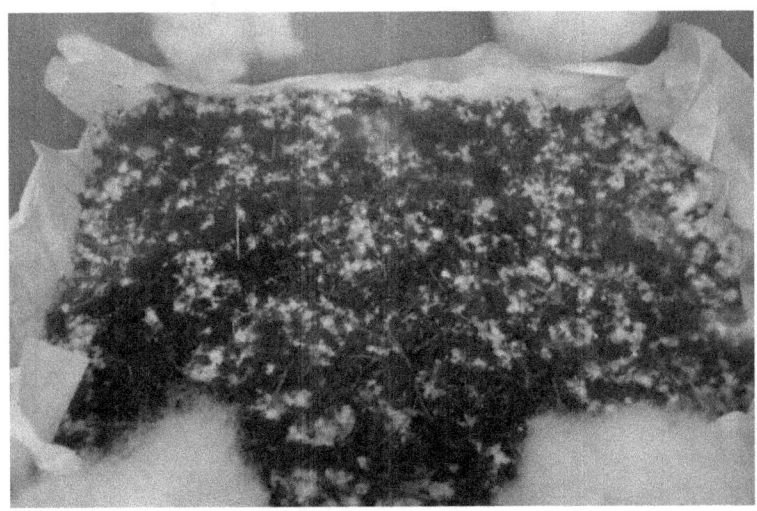

The monotub should be fully colonized within a few weeks. When fully colonized, the top layer of substrate should be completely covered with mycelium. Keep a look out for discolorations, quick growing fuzz, or a funky smell as this could mean the tub is contaminated.

Once fully colonized, the monotub is ready to start fruiting. If you put a trash bag over the top layer of the spawn and substrate cake during colonization, remove it once the top layer is fully covered with mycelium.

Step Six — Fruiting:

Within a few days to possibly weeks (depending on species and conditions), you should start seeing pins form on the top of the mycelium cake. These pins should mature rather quickly into full sized fruits. Depending on the type of mushroom, pins should become fully mature within a few days to a week's time.

Step Seven — Harvesting

The method of harvesting the fruits may vary a bit depending on the type of mushroom you are growing. Generally, you'll harvest by pinching the mushrooms at the base and gently twisting them from the cake. Do this for each individual or clump of fruits until you have removed them all. It is also possible to cut them at the base with a sharp blade, but using this method will leave a small amount of the fruit on the cake which may be prone to rot and cause contamination.

Store the mushrooms that you intend to use soon after harvesting in your fridge. Put them in a breathable container to prevent them from rotting too quickly. For long-term storage, freeze or dry the fruits.

Step Seven — Later Flushes:

After the first harvest, the monotub is still capable of producing quite a few more mushrooms. The average monotub will give you around three flushes, but, in some cases, it's possible to get six or seven. Each subsequent flush will be smaller than the last, so judge by the size of a flush whether or not waiting for another is worth the effort.

Once the mycelium has weakened and its food and moisture have run low, it will be vulnerable to contamination. So after the first couple of flushes, keep an eye out for any discoloration or other signs of mold growth. If you see mold, discard the cake and sterilize the monotub immediately to prevent contaminating the grow space.

Mushroom Grow Bag

Mushroom grow bags are a cheap and easy method for growing a wide variety of species. Not only can they be used as a self-contained fruiting environment, but they're also great for making a large quantity of spawn for use in other growing techniques.

A mushroom grow bag is a polypropylene bag that has a filter patch attached to it to assist with fresh air exchange while keeping contaminants out. The bags are gusseted, allowing them to expand and hold a good amount of substrate or spawn.

They're autoclavable as well, meaning they can withstand the high temperatures necessary for sterilization in a pressure cooker. This means the bag won't melt unless it is kept at a temperature of 266° to 340° Fahrenheit for an extended period of time. This makes them the ideal candidates for sterilizing a large quantity of grain or wood substrate at the standard 15 PSI.

These bags can be found for rather cheap online, or you can build one yourself (although since they are inexpensive, buying is preferrable). The bags have several uses for the home mushroom cultivator. You can use a mushroom grow bag as a spawn bag, to make fruiting blocks, to pasteurize a large amount of bulk substrate, or as a self-contained fruiting chamber.

When using the bag as a fruiting chamber, the top of the bag creates a humidity dome, while the mushrooms will spawn from the colonized block of substrate that's at the base. The main issue with this is lack of fresh air exposure, so when fruiting in a bag, it'll need to be opened and fanned regularly.

The main drawback to using a mushroom grow bag is the lack of reusability. While it is possible to reuse them for other purposes (as long as you don't have to cut the bag), you'll eventually need to discard it. When using mason jars and a fruiting chamber like a monotube, everything can be used repeatedly. Buying new bags for each grow isn't too costly though, but it's definitely not environmentally friendly.

While there are several different ways to use a mushroom grow bag, below we'll cover how to create a fruiting block that can grow a large quantity of fruits:

Necessary Materials:

- Mushroom grow bag with 0.2 to 0.5 micron filter patch
- Substrate (to make a ~5-pound block) will include:
    - 5 cups of hardwood pellets
    - 1.4 liters of water
    - 1.25 cups of wheat bran
- Mushroom spawn, liquid culture, or a colonized agar plate
- Gloves
- Zip ties
- Tyvek material (either Tyvek envelopes from the post office or a piece of a Tyvek painter's suit)
- 70% isopropyl alcohol
- Bleach solution (10% bleach, 90% water)
- Perlite

Necessary Tools:

- Pressure cooker
- Glove box
- Large mixing container (plastic storage bin or large bowl)
- Measuring cup
- Strainer

Fruiting Chamber:

- Shotgun fruiting chamber

Step One — Prepare the Substrate:

First, you need to gather all the materials and measure them out. For a five-pound block (if you're adding around 12oz of mushroom spawn, results will vary if inoculating using another source) you'll need five cups of hardwood pellets, 1.4 liters of water, and 1.25 cups of wheat bran.

Once everything is measured, first add the hardwood pellets to the mixing container. Next, add the water to the pellets and mix until the pellets are broken up. Using warm water will speed up this process. Make sure all the pellets are broken up as this will allow the mycelium to colonize the substrate quicker.

On top of the pellet and water mixture, add the wheat bran. The bran will work as an additional nutrient source for the mycelium. Don't add too much bran as it's also a great nutrient source for contaminants such as mold, so too much will increase the risk of contamination. Mix all the ingredients thoroughly.

Step Two — Put Substrate Into Grow Bag:

Add the mixture you prepared in the last step to the grow bag. If you're preparing enough substrate to use in multiple grow bags, you'll want to weigh out the correct amount of the mixture.

For a five-pound block, add four pounds and four ounces of substrate to the bag. Avoid getting any substrate on the sides of the bag, as contaminants can use this nutrient source as a pathway to contaminate the block later.

Step Three — Insert Tyvek Filter:

Now, you should put a piece of Tvek in front of the filter patch on the grow bag. This is done to help prevent contaminated air from entering the bag during the cooldown process after sterilization.

To insert the filter, cut a piece of Tyvek (either from a painter's suit found at a hardware store, or from Tyvek envelopes which can be obtained for free from the post office) to the correct size to slide between the gussets on the sides of the bag. Once the Tyvek is inserted, fold it over until it lays flat along the top of the substrate block.

Step Four — Sterilize:

Now, get the pressure cooker and make sure it has the metal rack intended for canning along the bottom (jar lids will also work). Pour about two inches of water along the bottom of the cooker. Place the folded over mushroom grow bag/-s into the pressure cooker.

Put a plate, or something else heavy and heat resistant on top of the bag. This is a vital step, as it will keep the bag from expanding during the sterilization process and blocking the pressure release valve. If this valve is blocked, it could potentially be dangerous, so don't skip this step.

Seal the lid back onto the pressure cooker and put it onto the stove at high heat. Wait until the cooker reaches 15 PSI, and then adjust the heat to keep it at this pressure level. Cook the bags for about two and a half hours to fully sterilize the block. It is necessary to cook the bags for this length of time because of the size and density of the block. You want to ensure that the heat kills everything into the center.

After heating the bag/-s at 15 PSI for two and a half hours, remove the pressure cooker from the heat. Allow the pressure cooker to sit undisturbed for at least 8 hours to give it a chance to cool and for the internal pressure to return to normal.

Step Five — Inoculate the Substrate:

Before you inoculate the substrate block, make certain that it has completely cooled down. If it's too hot, you will kill the mycelium in the spawn and ruin the fruiting block. Now, prepare the glove box by wiping it down with a 10% bleach solution using a clean rag or paper towel. Place the substrate block into the glove box.

Put on your gloves and sterilize your hands using the isopropyl alcohol. If you're inoculating using mushroom spawn, open the bag and quickly add 12oz of spawn, then seal it with a zip tie. If using agar, or liquid culture, follow the same process but add the alternate inoculant source instead. Once sealed, shake up the bag to evenly distribute the spawn and speed up the colonization process.

Step Six — Wait for Colonization:

Find a place that gets ambient light but no direct sunlight and put the bag there to colonize. Full colonization should take anywhere from 10 to 21 days. However, colonization times may vary depending on the species you're growing, the type of substrate being used, how much substrate is in each bag, and other environmental factors.

Regularly check the grow bag for signs of contamination. Contaminations can take the form of discoloration, such as a red, green, or wispy gray area, or as a wet slimy looking spot. If you believe the bag is contaminated, do not open it! Opening a contaminated bag can taint the grow area, so it's best to just throw the whole bag away.

Once the bag is fully colonized, you will have a large block of spawn that can be used for fruiting or to inoculate other grow bags. If you would like to fruit the block, follow the next steps.

Step Seven — Prepare the Fruiting Chamber:

For a bag grow, a large shotgun fruiting chamber will provide an ideal fruiting environment. First, sterilize the fruiting chamber using a 10% bleach solution or isopropyl alcohol. Next, wet some perlite to field capacity using a large strainer.

Line the bottom of the shotgun fruiting chamber with about 3" to 4" of wet perlite. This will keep the fruiting environment nice and humid.

Step Eight — Fruiting:

Once the outside of the bag is completely covered with mycelium, wait a few more days for it to fully consolidate before you fruit. Depending on the type of mushroom you're growing, there are different ways to go about fruiting. If you want the mushrooms to grow from the side of the bag, as is the case for lion's mane, cut Xs into the bag and the fruits will sprout from there. For mushrooms you would like to grow from the top of the bag, cut off the top portion of the bag.

Regardless of how you're growing the fruits, you'll need to introduce them to a humid environment to initiate fruiting. For the at-home cultivator, a shotgun fruiting chamber is an easy solution. Place the cut bag into the prepped fruiting chamber and close the lid. Fan the fruiting chamber several times a day, or have an electric fan blowing on it at a low power setting to ensure proper fresh air exposure (fresh air exposure is more important with some species than it is with others).

After about one to two weeks, depending on conditions and the strain you're growing, you should see pins begin to form on the block. These pins should expand into full-sized fruits within about one week's time.

Step Nine — Harvesting:

Once the fruits are mature, but before they've begun dropping spores, it's time to fruit. For collecting the fruits, you can remove the block from the fruiting chamber for easy access. Remove the mushrooms by gripping them at the base and gently twisting them from the block. It's also possible to cut them as close to the base as possible using a sharp knife or razor blade.

For fruits that you intend to use within a relatively short period of time, store them in the fridge in a breathable container. Using an airtight container will cause them to rot quickly. If you want to store them long-term, freezing them or drying them is preferred.

Step Ten — Later Flushes

The good thing about growing using this method is that you can get quite a few flushes from the fruiting block. Depending on the amount of substrate used, you can easily get three to five flushes from a single block.

Each flush will be smaller than the previous flush, so use the size of the current flush to determine whether waiting for another would be worth your time. Additionally, after around three flushes, the mycelium of the block will be more prone to contaminants such as mold. Mold spores in the fruiting environment can cause problems with future grows, so allowing the block to flush too many times does pose some risk.

Outdoor Bed Using Straw Logs

Not only are outdoor mushroom beds fun to watch grow, but they offer some real advantages over the oxygen starved indoor fruiting chamber alternatives. Mushrooms grown outdoors will grow larger, often give better yields, and can even look completely different.

Species such as reishi and king oyster mushrooms will grow very differently when given an oxygen-rich environment like an outdoor bed or log. Some species will also have a better texture and even a slightly different flavor when grown in an outdoor bed.

Creating an outdoor bed is also relatively easy and requires little maintenance. Things like sterility and a clean work environment aren't nearly as important when growing in the great outdoors. These beds will also produce fruits year after year whenever the right conditions are met as long as you keep them topped up with a suitable food source or substrate.

The main downside to growing mushrooms in an outdoor bed is exposure to the elements. When growing indoors, it's easy to protect the grow from pests, control the temperature, and keep humidity at the optimum levels. Outdoors, an unexpected heat wave or unusually cold night could cause problems. Additionally, birds and insects may feed on the fruits and there's little you can do about it.

Nonetheless, the advantages to having a beautiful outdoor bed of mushrooms you can harvest each season far outweigh the risks. So if you have a suitable yard or other outdoor space to grow in, this is an excellent option.

The method below is great for a variety of oyster mushroom species. To make an outdoor bed using a straw log, take the following steps:

Necessary Materials:

- Wheat or oat straw or already colonized straw log
- Mushroom grain spawn
- A large container for pasteurization (large plastic storage container works well)
- Pillowcase
- Gloves
- 70% isopropyl alcohol or bleach solution (10% bleach and 90% water)
- 16" poly tubing or plastic bag
- Peat moss
- Garden soil

Necessary Tools:

- String trimmer for chopping straw
- Candy thermometer
- Shovel

Step One — Chop the Straw:

The first thing you need to do is prepare the straw by chopping it into smaller pieces. It's possible to do this using a pair of gardening shears, but the easiest way to get the straw down to size is to use a string trimmer (weed whacker).

You want the straw to be chopped into 1" to 3" pieces. To do this, put the straw in a large barrel or drum, place the string trimmer into the drum, turn it on, and chop. The size of each piece of straw doesn't need to be precise, just make sure it's all chopped up fairly well.

Once chopped, it's a good idea (but not necessary) to soak the straw with a bit of dish soap for a few hours to help kill any bacteria that may be living on it. After soaking, give the straw a thorough washing.

Step Two — Pasteurize the Straw:

Pasteurizing the straw is necessary to minimize the likelihood of contamination once the straw has been inoculated. To pasteurize the straw, first stuff it all into a large pillowcase. Put the pillowcase into a large plastic storage container and fill it with boiling water. Place something heavy on the pillowcase to make sure it stays submerged in the water.

You'll want to keep the water in the container at about 160° Fahrenheit for one to two hours. Use a candy thermometer to check the temperature of the water, and when it falls below 160° Fahrenheit, add more boiling water to the storage container.

After about one to two hours, let the water cool down to room temperature and remove the pillowcase. Allow the excess water to drain from the pillowcase and let it cool completely before moving on to the next step.

Step Three — Mix Mushroom Grain Spawn and Straw

Now, it's time to inoculate the straw by adding colonized grain spawn to it. Put the pasteurized straw back into the plastic storage container. Make sure the container is clean, so a quick wipe down with 70% isopropyl alcohol or a 10% bleach solution will ensure it's contaminant free.

Add the mushroom grain spawn to the straw at a ratio of 15% spawn and 85% straw. Mix the straw and the spawn thoroughly. It's a good idea to wear clean gloves when doing this. Use your gloved hands to mix the straw and grain spawn until the two are evenly distributed. Do not mix in the spawn until the straw is completely cooled. If the straw is still too hot it can kill the mycelium living in the spawn.

Step Four — Stuff Spawn and Straw Mix Into Poly Tubing:

Once you've properly mixed the substrate and straw together, it's time to form the "logs." To do this, you're going to need to stuff the inoculated straw into either a long plastic bag (something like a small, clear trash bag will work), or poly tubing. If using poly tubing, buy a roll with a 16" lay flat diameter. The trash bag should be of a similar diameter.

With poly tubing, you'll first need to zip tie one end shut before stuffing the mix. Now, stuff the inoculated substrate into the tube or bag one handful at a time. Use clean gloves when doing this step. As you go, pack the mix in tightly with your hands to prevent air pockets.

Do this until the log is of the desired length (somewhere around 2' to 4' should suffice). Once you've added enough inoculated substrate, twist the top of the bag or tubing to help pack in the material as tightly as possible. Tie the open end off with a zip tie and set the tube aside. Repeat this process for as many logs as you intend to make. The number of logs you make will depend on the size of the outdoor bed.

After the tubes are complete, use an alcohol sterilized razor to cut Xs about 5" apart around the whole bag. This will allow the mycelium to breathe as it colonizes. When it's fully colonized, these holes may begin to fruit. This is fine; allow the fruits to mature and harvest them. The colonized log can still be used for your outdoor bed. If you're hanging the log during colonization, punch some holes in the bottom of the plastic to allow excess moisture to drain.

Step Five — Wait for Colonization:

Move the prepared bag containing the inoculated substrate to a suitable area for colonization. It should be someplace that's out of direct sunlight, but still receives some indirect light and is at a normal room temperature. If it's an option, you can hang the bag as this will allow excess moisture to drain freely. The log should colonize within one to four weeks depending on size and temperature.

Every few days, check the bag for contaminants. For mold, look for abnormal wispy grey growths or discoloration, such as a red or green spot. A bacterial contamination will cause the log to smell bad and create slimy looking wet spots. If you spot a contamination, discard the bag without opening it to prevent spreading spores throughout your colonization area.

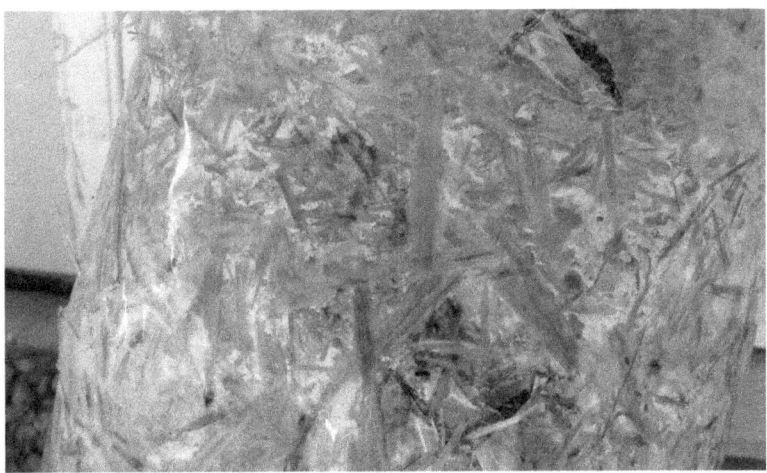

Once the log is fully colonized, it's ready for the outdoor bed. Alternatively, you could leave it as is and fruits will grow from the holes you cut in the previous step (although fruiting conditions should be introduced if opting for this method).

Step Six — Select a Space to Make Your Outdoor Bed:

Your outdoor bed should be in an area that receives a lot of shade and is out of direct sunlight. Under a tree, on the side of a house, or near a large bush could all work. The larger your bed, the more straw logs you'll need to make. Two logs should be adequate for a 3' by 6' bed.

Step Seven — Cut the Colonized Logs Into Disks:

Now, you're going to break the logs into disks that will fill the space you intend to use for the outdoor bed. These disks should be around 2" to 3" thick, but these measurements do not need to be too precise. If the log has already developed fruits, make sure to remove all of the remaining pins and mushrooms from the log.

If you would like to create flat edges to fully fill in the garden, you can break the disks in half. Breaking them into smaller pieces to fill any large holes left between the disks is also fine. Just make sure to fill the bed in as best as possible with the colonized straw.

Step Eight — Cover Disks With a Casing Layer:

First, you're going to want to make the casing layer. The casing layer should be a material that doesn't have any nutrients. An ideal mix for the casing layer is 50% peat moss and 50% dirt or garden soil. The casing layer will help the bed to stay moist and prevent the straw disks from drying out.

Place the peat moss and soil into a large container and mix thoroughly. Next, add water to the casing layer until it reaches field capacity. You'll know it's at field capacity when picking up a handful and squeezing it only causes a small stream of water to pour out from it, but when holding it, no water drips from the mix.

Using a shovel, cover the top of the colonized disks with the casing layer. Make sure that the casing is evenly distributed across the bed. The casing layer doesn't need to be too thick. A layer of about 2" should be fine.

Step Nine — Maintain the Outdoor Bed:

It's important that you do not let the outdoor bed completely dry out as this could kill the mycelium. To keep it moist, water the bed every day or two, depending on weather conditions and sun exposure.

Just check the outdoor bed daily and see if it looks dry. If the top casing layer looks like it is beginning to dry out, give it a light misting. Do not spray too much water onto the bed. If it becomes too waterlogged you will increase the risk of contamination and limit the amount of air that can reach the mycelium.

Step Ten — Fruiting:

Depending on weather conditions, you should begin to see the first pins springing up from your garden within a few weeks. These pins should expand into full-size fruits in a relatively short period of time. On average, they should mature in about one week.

Step Eleven — Harvesting:

You can harvest each individual mushroom once it has reached the appropriate size. Pick them once they are about full sized and before they have begun dropping their spores. The longer you wait to harvest, the more likely they are to become infested with insects, such as fungus gnats, or be eaten by other pests.

To harvest the mushrooms, pinch them at the base and gently twist them from the ground. More mushrooms should continue to grow throughout the grow season. Harvest each flush as soon as the fruits mature. Each year, you may continue to get fruits from the outdoor bed. More straw can be added under the casing layer to reinvigorate the mycelium and give it extra nutrients.

For short term storage, keep the mushrooms in the fridge in a breathable container to prevent rot. If you intend to store them for a longer period of time, it's possible to freeze or to dry the fruits.

Chapter Six: Advanced Techniques

Agar

For anyone who gets into the hobby of home mushroom cultivation, agar is a great tool that can be used for a variety of purposes. Agar is ideal for things like cloning a mushroom with desirable traits, inoculating spawn, or making liquid cultures.

Agar is derived from red algae and is a red gelatinous substance. It's used in a variety of desserts in Asia as well as to grow bacterial and fungal cultures in microbiology. It's rich in nutrients, which makes it an ideal food source for a wide variety of microorganisms, including mushroom mycelium.

Making your own sterile agar plates is relatively easy. These plates can then be inoculated using a liquid culture, spores, a piece of mycelium, or live mushroom tissue (for cloning). There's a variety of different recipes you can use to make the agar, including malt-yeast agar, potato dextrose agar, or dog food agar. Malt extract agar is the most common recipe used by most mushroom cultivators.

Agar can often be found in Asian markets and is widely found online as well. The other ingredients needed for the agar plates are also easily found in grocery stores or across the web.

Making Sterilized Malt Extract Agar Plates

To make sterilized malt extract agar plates that are ready to inoculate, take the following steps:

Necessary Materials:

- 20 grams of agar (for 1000ml of water)
- 20 grams of light malt extract (for 1000ml of water)
- 2 grams of nutritional yeast (for 1000ml of water)
- 1000ml water
- Sterile agar plates
- Bottle capable of pressure cooking
- Poly-fill
- Aluminum foil
- Gloves
- 70% isopropyl alcohol
- Bleach solution (10% bleach and 90% water) or Lysol
- Lab parafilm

Necessary Tools:

- Pressure cooker
- Hammer
- Large nail
- Measuring cup
- Block of wood
- Funnel
- Glove box

Step One — Modify Bottle Lid:

Find a bottle that's capable of withstanding the heat of a pressure cooker. A glass bottle with a metal lid is ideal. Something like an old whisky or olive oil bottle is perfect, just make sure it doesn't have any elements that will melt when you sterilize it in the cooker.

To modify the lid for gas exchange during sterilization, you'll need to create a hole in it and block it with something breathable. A good way to do this is to place the lid, flat side down, onto an old block of wood. Hammer a large nail through the lid to create the hole and remove the nail. Stuff poly-fill through the hole to fill it. Cut away the excess poly-fill.

Step Two — Mix Ingredients:

To mix the ingredients, you must first mix the dry ingredients, adding 20 grams of malt extract, 20 grams of agar, and 2 grams of nutritional yeast. Using a funnel will make adding the ingredients to the bottle a lot easier. Shake them to mix the ingredients well. Measure out and add 1000ml of hot tap water to the dry ingredients and mix well by swirling the bottle. Avoid using cold water as this will make mixing more difficult and cause the agar to set early.

Once all the materials are mixed, screw on the modified lid from step one. Take a small square of aluminum foil and cover the lid.

Step Three — Sterilize Agar Mix:

Put a canning rack into the pressure cooker to prevent the bottle from coming into direct contact with the bottom as it cooks. If you don't have a canning rack, the rings from mason jar bottles will work.

Put the bottle containing the agar mix into the pressure cooker. You can use empty mason jars to support the bottle to ensure it stays upright while cooking. To prevent the agar from boiling over, which occurs if the bottle cools faster than the agar within it, fill the pressure cooker with water until it reaches the same level as the agar within the bottle. This will make sure that the bottle cools at the same rate as the agar within it.

Seal the lid onto the pressure cooker and place it on the stove at high heat. Once the cooker reaches 15 PSI, lower the heat to keep it at this pressure level. Cook the agar at 15 PSI for 45 minutes.

Step Four — Allow Pressure Cooker to Cool:

During this step, it's important that you allow the pressure cooker to cool enough to return to normal pressure, but don't cool the agar too much, as you don't want it to set. Around two hours of cooling should be sufficient for this. Prepare the pouring area while waiting for the cooker to cool.

Step Five — Prepare Agar Plates for Pouring:

When pouring the agar plates, keeping everything sterile is absolutely essential. You should wear gloves that you wipe down with 70% isopropyl alcohol often, as well as wear clean clothes. You can also wear a surgical mask if you have one.

While waiting for the pressure cooker to cool, prepare the pouring area by wiping everything down with Lysol or a 10% bleach solution. Do the same for the glove box, which is where you'll do the actual pouring. Wearing your gloves and clean clothes, put the sterile agar plates or mason jars into the glove box.

Sterile agar plates can be bought online or in a lab supply shop. Make sure to leave the plates closed until the actual pouring and wipe the outside surface with 70% isopropyl alcohol right before putting them into the glove box. If the plates are in a sterile bag, wipe down the bag with alcohol and open it from the bottom in the glove box to remove the stacked plates.

Step Six — Pour the Agar:

When it's safe to open the pressure cooker, remove the bottle and move it into the clean glove box as quickly as possible. Use alcohol wiped gloved hands for this. If the bottle is exposed to the open air for any significant amount of time, wipe it down with alcohol right before putting it in the box.

To pour the agar, remove the foil from the lid and open the jar. Starting from the bottom of the stacked agar plates, pour the agar into the plate using just enough to completely cover its bottom. Replace the lid to the plate as quickly as possible and make sure not to touch the inside of the plate. Repeat this process for each plate. Allow the plates to cool and solidify within the glove box.

Step Seven — Storing Plates:

Once the plates have completely cooled, they're ready to be inoculated. However, if you plan to store them for long-term use, you will want to seal them to prevent contamination. To seal the plates, use lab parafilm which can be easily purchased online.

Take a piece of lab parafilm that's around 4" in length and remove the paper from its backside. Fold the film in half and wrap it tightly around the diameter of the plate. Do this as tightly as possible to ensure the film sticks to the plate.

No Pour Agar Technique

Necessary Materials:

- 8oz (250ml) wide mouth mason jars with lids or polypropylene PP5 plastic deli cups with PP5 lids (if PP5 they're safe to sterilize in a pressure cooker)
- 10 grams of agar (for 500ml water)
- 10 grams of light malt extract

- 500ml water
- Wide mouth synthetic filter discs (sized to fit wide mouth mason jars)
- Aluminum foil

Necessary Tools:

- Pressure cooker
- Power drill
- 5/16" drill bit
- Block of wood
- Measuring cup
- Cooking pot

Step One — Prepare Jar Lids:

To prepare the jar lids, place the center disks from the mason jar lids onto an old block of wood that you don't mind drilling into. Drill two holes using a 5/16" drill bit into the center of each lid about 1" to 2" apart. This will help to prevent the agar from boiling over later on.

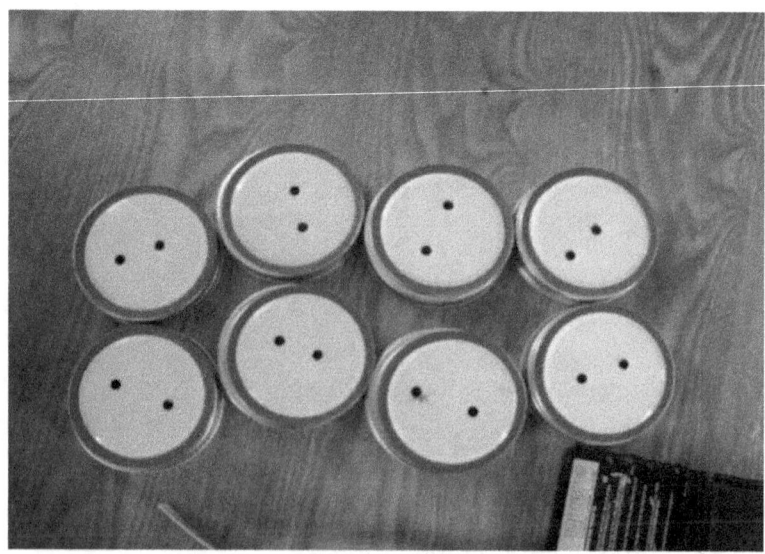

Step Two — Cook the Agar:

Measure out 500ml of cold water using a measuring cup and pour it into the cooking pot. Add 10 grams of light malt extract and 10 grams of agar to the cold water. The dry ingredients will not dissolve into the cold water at first, but will melt upon cooking.

Place your pot containing the ingredients on the stove and bring it to a light simmer. As the water heats, the agar and light malt extract will dissolve into the water. Simmer the ingredients for about three to five minutes or until the ingredients have melted.

Step Three — Preparing Jars:

Take the agar mix on the stove and pour around 60ml of the solution into each jar. Put the center plate of the lid prepared in step one onto the jar with the bottom side facing upwards and the metal top side touching the glass. Place the filter disks on top of the upside down jar lid.

Now, take the rings used to seal the center plate of the jar lid and screw them on loosely over both the filter disk and the lid. Cover each lid with aluminum foil.

Step Four — Sterilize Agar Jars:

Put a canning rack into the pressure cooker to prevent the jars from touching the bottom during cooking. If you don't have a canning rack, line the bottom of the cooker with the rings from mason jar lids. This will prevent the jars from breaking during the cooking process.

Load the jars into the pressure cooker and add water. Fill with water until it reaches a level of about 5mm above the bottom of the jars. Seal the lid onto the pressure cooker. Place the pressure cooker onto the stove at high heat until it reaches 15 PSI. Once the proper pressure is reached, lower the heat to maintain 15 PSI for 45 minutes. Remove the pressure cooker from the heat after the time has passed.

Step Five — Allow to Cool:

Allow the pressure cooker containing the jars to cool for at least eight hours. Sterilizing at night and allowing it to cool until morning is ideal. Once cooled, the agar will be set and ready for inoculation.

Inoculating Agar

Necessary Materials:

- Prepared agar plates
- Liquid culture syringe or spore syringe
- 70% isopropyl alcohol
- Bleach solution (10% bleach and 90% water) or Lysol
- Gloves

Necessary Tools:

- Glove box
- Bunsen burner or lighter

Step One — Prepare Glove Box:

First, clean the area you're going to be working in using the 10% bleach solution or Lysol. Place the glove box in the working area and wipe the inside with the bleach solution or Lysol as well.

Take the prepared agar plates and wipe each one down with 70% isopropyl alcohol and immediately load them into the glove box. Make sure to wear gloves when placing anything into the glove box and regularly wipe your gloved hands down with 70% isopropyl alcohol.

Step Two — Inoculate the Agar:

Put on gloves and use alcohol to sterilize your gloved hands. Heat the metal needle of your syringe until glowing hot using either a Bunsen burner or a lighter. Put your gloved hands into the glove box with the syringe.

Quickly remove the lid of the agar plate and squirt a small amount of either spores or liquid culture into the center of the plate. Do not touch the plate with the syringe. Put the lid back onto the agar plate as quickly as possible. One CC should be enough for about three agar plates. It's also possible to inoculate the plates with a small sliver of colonized agar cut from another plate or live mushroom tissue (more on this later in the cloning section).

Step Three — Wait for Colonization:

Place the agar plates in a clean area that's out of direct sunlight to colonize. The time it takes to colonize will vary depending on whether you used a liquid culture or spores. Spores can take up to two weeks to germinate, while a liquid culture will start spreading within a few days.

Once you see the first signs of mycelial growth, the plate should be ready to use within 7 to 14 days. The rate of growth depends on how aggressive the genetics of the mycelium is, the strain you're growing, and environmental conditions.

Your colonized agar plate can be used to inoculate a liquid culture, grain, sawdust, or any other suitable substrate.

Self-Healing Injection Port Lids

When making a liquid culture, spore syringes, or mushroom spawn, using self-healing injection port lids are ideal. The lids consist of a hole covered with high temperature silicon that you can inject spores or liquid culture through, and another hole that's covered with a filter for gas exchange. Self-healing injection port lids can also be purchased through mushroom cultivation websites.

DIY Self-Healing Injection Port Lids

Necessary Materials:

- Mason jar lids
- High-temperature RTV silicone
- ¼" plumbing inserts
- Poly-fill

- Tyvek (from painter's coveralls or postal service tyvek mailers)
- Micropore tape

Necessary Tools:

- Power drill
- ¼" drill bit
- Pliers
- Block of wood

Step One — Drill Lids:

First, place the circular center inserts from the mason jar lids onto a block of wood that you don't mind drilling through. Drill two ¼" holes into the lids across from one another on opposites sides.

Step Two — Make Injection Port:

Take the RVT high-temperature silicone and fill one of the holes with it. Apply the silicone to both sides of the hole to make sure it's fully blocked. Take two small squares of paper and sandwich the wet silicone between them to make it nice and flat.

Allow the silicone to cure for 24 hours sandwiched between the paper. Remove the paper once it's cured. Hot water can help you remove any paper that's stuck to the silicone.

Step Three — Create Gas Exchange Port:

Put the plumbing insert through the second hole. Seal it in place as close to flush with the top of the lid as possible using the RVT high-temperature silicone. Apply silicone around the bottom of the insert as well to make sure it's completely sealed. Allow the silicone to cure for 24 hours.

Once the silicon is dry and the plumbing insert is firmly attached to the lid, stuff the insert with poly-fill. Crimp the bottom end of the insert together as best as possible using a pair of pliers. This step will keep the poly-fill from getting wet and help to prevent contamination from entering the jar. Using micropore tape, attach a small square of Tyvek over the top side of the plumbing insert.

Step Four — Use the Lid:

To use the lid, simply attach it to the mason jar using the ring portion of the lid. Due to the high-temperature silicone used, this lid can be pressure cooked over and over again, making it easy to sterilize. Using a syringe, you can inject both spores and liquid culture through the silicone injection port. This will make it far easier to prevent contaminations when making a liquid culture or inoculating grains.

Liquid Culture

Like agar, making a liquid culture is a technique you can use to grow mycelium to inoculate a suitable food source for mushroom growth, such as grain or agar. There are quite a few advantages to using a liquid culture.

First, they can be put into a syringe to make inoculating jars through an inoculation point to make keeping the process sterile much easier. It will also make colonization times much faster than using spores. On top of this, liquid cultures can be stored for quite a long time in a cold environment like the fridge.

To make a liquid culture, all you need to do is create a water solution called a "broth." The broth is simply a combination of water and a nutrient source. A wide variety of different nutrient sources can be used, including honey, corn syrup, malt extract, grain water, or brown rice flour water just to name some of the options.

Making a Liquid Culture

Necessary Materials:

- Spore syringe or liquid culture syringe
- ½ pint, pint, or quart mason jar (depends on how much you intend to make)
- Self-healing injection port lids
- Distilled water (600ml for quart mason jar, 300ml for pint jar, and 150ml for ½ pint jar)
- Karo light corn syrup (12ml for quart mason jar, 6ml for pint jar, and 3ml for ½ pint jar)
- Extra light dry malt extract (1.2 grams for quart mason jar, 0.6 grams for pint jar, 0.3 grams for ½ pint jar)
- Aluminum foil
- Gloves
- 70% isopropyl alcohol
- Bleach solution (10% bleach and 90% water) or Lysol
- Sterile 10CC syringes with 16-gauge needles

Necessary Tools:

- Pressure cooker
- Glove box
- Gram scale (for measuring malt extract)

- Oral syringe (for measuring ml of karo)
- Measuring cup
- Bunsen burner or lighter

Step One — Combine Ingredients:

For simplicity, I'll include the measurements needed if you are using a pint mason jar in these instructions, so adjust accordingly if using a different sized jar.

Start by measuring out 300ml of cold distilled water using the measuring cup. With the oral syringe, measure out 6ml of light corn syrup and weigh out 0.6 grams of light dry malt extract using a gram scale. Place all these ingredients into a jar and mix well.

Next, microwave the jar containing the ingredients until they're mostly dissolved. It's not necessary to get the water to boiling; you only need to heat the water enough for almost everything to dissolve. Once the ingredients are dissolved and the water is clear, allow the mixture to settle for about a minute.

After it settles, you may have some sediment left on the bottom of the jar. Pour most of the mixture into the jar you'll be using for the liquid culture, being careful to leave the remaining sediment in the first jar. The easiest way to do this is to leave just a bit of the liquid culture broth containing the sediment in the first jar.

Step Two — Sterilize Broth:

Place a canning rack along the bottom Take the pressure cooker and place a canning rack along the bottom. If you don't have a canning rack, line the bottom with the rings used for mason jar lids. This will prevent the jar from touching the bottom and breaking during the sterilization process.

Screw the self-healing injection port lid onto the jar containing the broth you made for the liquid culture. Cover the lid with aluminum foil to prevent moisture from getting into the gas exchange hole. Place the jar upright in the pressure cooker. Pour about 1" to 2" of tap water into the pressure cooker and seal the lid onto it.

Put the pressure cooker on the stove at high heat and allow it to get to 15 PSI. Once the correct pressure is reached, lower the heat so that it maintains this level of pressure during the course of the sterilization process. Cook the jar at 15 PSI for 30 minutes before removing the pressure cooker from the heat. Allow the pressure cooker to cool for at least 8 hours before removing the jar.

Step Three — Inoculate the Liquid Culture

To inoculate the culture, first clean the area where you plan to work using a bleach solution or Lysol. Now, put the glove box into the workspace and wipe it down with the bleach solution or Lysol as well.

Take the jar containing the broth and quickly load it into the glove box directly from the pressure cooker. If the jar is exposed to air for a significant amount of time, wipe it down with alcohol. Wear gloves that have been wiped down with alcohol whenever you put your hands into the glove box.

Put on gloves and make sure to wipe them down with alcohol frequently during the inoculation. Get the syringe containing either spores or a liquid culture and heat the needle using a Bunsen burner or lighter until it is glowing red. Wipe the injection port on the jar with an alcohol soaked paper towel. Quickly stab the sterilized needle through the injection port and squirt about 1CC of either spores or liquid culture into the broth.

Step Four — Wait for Colonization:

If you used spores to inoculate the liquid culture, you may not see mycelium growth for up to two weeks. With a liquid culture inoculation, mycelium should become visible within a few days.

Mycelium will appear as a cloudy blob floating in the liquid. After the first signs of growth, the liquid culture should be ready to use within 7 to 14 days, depending on strain and environmental conditions.

Once the jar has a substantial amount of mycelial growth, it can be kept in the fridge for long-term storage. The cool environment of the fridge will slow the mycelial growth so it won't consume all the nutrients in the culture too quickly allowing for extended life.

Step Five — Make Liquid Culture Syringes:

To make liquid culture syringes, first clean a work area and the glove box using a bleach solution or Lysol. Next, gently shake and swirl the jar to break up the ball of mycelium floating in it; you want to break the ball into the smallest possible pieces, so that they can easily be sucked into a syringe.

Once the mycelium is somewhat broken up and small pieces are floating around the culture, wipe the jar down with alcohol and load it into the glove box while wearing clean gloves. Wipe your gloves down again and load the sterile syringes and needles into the glove box.

If using new syringes and needles, they will come in sterile packaging. Leave the packages unopened until you're ready to load them with culture. Wipe the packages down with alcohol before putting them in the glove box. Some syringes can be reused if they can withstand the heat of a pressure cooker for sterilization, however, new syringes are preferred.

Now, wearing gloves that have been freshly wiped down with alcohol, open the first syringe packaging in the glove box. Attach the 16-gauge needle while leaving the plastic needle guard on. Wipe the injection port of the jar with alcohol, remove the plastic needle guard, and quickly stab the needle through the injection port to suck up the liquid culture.

Swirling the jar a bit and tilting it right before sucking up the culture will help to ensure the small mycelium pieces are floating and are sucked into the syringe. Repeat this process with as many syringes as you intend to make. Store the liquid culture syringes in the fridge where they should be good for at least one year. These syringes can be used to inoculate everything from grain, to agar, to other liquid cultures.

Spore Prints

Every mushroom you grow is capable of producing more than a billion spores. These spores can be collected and used for future grows. You can use a single spore print to make between 10 to 20 spore syringes. This means that after the first grow, realistically, you may never have to buy another spore syringe for as long as you live.

Making spore prints is a relatively easy process. These prints can be stored in a dry cool place potentially for years before they're no longer viable. Making spore prints from mushrooms that grow caps is easiest, and the technique for capless species such as morels or puffballs may vary from the steps covered below.

Aluminum Foil Spore Prints

Necessary Materials:

- Mushroom caps
- Jars
- Aluminum foil
- 70% isopropyl alcohol
- Bleach solution (10% bleach and 90% water)
- Gloves
- Plastic push pin thumb tacks
- Clean zip lock bags

Necessary Tools:

- Pressure cooker
- Glove box
- Sharp knife or razor blade
- Scissors

Step One — Cut Aluminum Squares and Sterilize Equipment:

To begin, cut out as many aluminum squares as you'll need for the number of spore prints you intend to make. Make sure the squares are large enough to fit the whole cap of the mushrooms you're using to make prints. Folding the foil squares in half and unfolding them before you've made the print will make the process of folding them easier later on after the spores have dropped onto the foil.

Load the foil squares into a jar and screw on the lid. Collect enough jars to cover each spore print you intend to make, and load everything into a pressure cooker. Make sure the cooker has either a canning rack or is lined with mason jar lid rings along the bottom to prevent jars from breaking. Pour about 2" of tap water into the pressure cooker and seal its lid.

Put the pressure cooker onto the stove on high heat until it reaches 15 PSI then lower the heat so it maintains this level of pressure. Cook everything for 45 minutes and remove the pressure cooker from the heat. Allow everything to cool for several hours.

Step Two — Prepare Work Area and Glove Box:

While you wait for the pressure cooker to cool, you can prepare the work area. To do this, clean the area well by wiping everything down with the bleach solution or Lysol. Wipe the interior of the glove box and its lid with disinfectant as well to kill off as many potential contaminants as possible.

Step Three — Load Glove Box:

Once the pressure cook has cooled, put on gloves and wipe them down with alcohol. Open the pressure cooker and load its contents directly into the glove box to minimize their exposure to outside air.

Wipe the gloves with alcohol one more time, and open the jar containing the aluminum squares. Lay the square flat along the bottom of the glove box and cover it with a jar, mouth side down. Do this for each aluminum square.

Step Four — Collect Mushroom Caps:

When choosing caps to collect for making prints, choose ones that are fully extended and about ready to drop their spores. Caps that have already begun dropping spores will work as well. Larger caps are preferable as they will provide a bigger print.

Once you've chosen the caps you want to take the prints from, insert a push pin thumb tack into the top center of each cap. Additionally, you can gently wipe a little alcohol on the top of the cap and thumb tack to kill potential contaminants.

Put on gloves and rub your hands down with alcohol. Take a razor blade or sharp knife and wipe it down with alcohol as well. With one hand, hold the thumb tack that's inserted into the cap, and use the other hand to cut the cap from the mushroom as close to the gills or pores as possible. Avoid touching the gills or pores of the mushroom when doing this.

Holding the thumb tack, bring the cap to the glove box and place it, gills down, on one of the aluminum squares. Do this as quickly as possible and be sure not to flip the cap gills side up to prevent mold spores or other contaminants from landing on it. Repeat this process for each cap and aluminum square.

Step Five — Wait for Spores to Drop and Dry Prints:

Once all of the caps are loaded under the jars, wait 12 to 24 hours for the spores to drop. The longer you wait the more spores you'll collect, but don't wait too long or the cap will begin to rot. Once 12 to 24 hours have passed you can remove the caps from the foil. Wear gloves that have been freshly wiped down with alcohol when removing the caps.

When you remove the cap, you should see a perfect spore print with the same design of the gills or pores of the mushroom you used to make it. The color of the spores will vary depending on the species of the mushroom, with some being far more visible than others.

Once the cap has been removed, replace the jar over the print and let it sit covered for another 24 hours to allow it to dry.

Step Six — Fold and Store Prints:

After the print has set to dry for 24 hours, put your gloves back on and wipe them down with alcohol. Reach into the glove box and remove the jar from the first print. Fold the print in half, and then fold again along the three open edges to seal it and protect it from outside air. Fold each open edge about 2mm in, just enough to seal it from air getting in.

Place the print in a clean zip lock bag, seal it, and label the bag with the date and species of mushroom. Repeat this process for each spore print. Store the prints in a cool dry place or in a refrigerator for long-term storage.

Spore Syringes

While it's possible to order already made spore syringes, it's much more economical to make your own. For about the price of one spore syringe, you can order a spore print from most mushroom cultivation websites. This print can be used to make 10 to 20 spore syringes. You'll need to buy syringes as well, but sterile syringes and needles can be found for pretty cheap on a variety of websites.

After the first grow, you can also make your own spore prints (process outlined in previous section) to make as many spore syringes as you'd like. Once you have this process down you can become your own self-contained mushroom growing factory.

There are a wide variety of methods for making your own spore syringes. The method I'll outline below is one of the easiest ways that anyone can do at home with minimal supplies.

DIY Spore Syringe

Necessary Materials:

- Sterile 10CC syringes with 16 gauge needles
- Spore print
- Distilled water
- Quart mason jars
- Self-healing injection port lid
- Gloves
- 70% isopropyl alcohol
- Bleach solution (10% bleach and 90% water) or Lysol
- Aluminum foil

Necessary Tools:

- Pressure cooker
- Glove box
- Inoculation loop (can be made using a piece of wire with a small loop folded onto one side)
- Shot glass or small jar

Step One — Sterilize Water and Equipment:

First, you need to make sure everything you're going to use for this process is sterile and free from contaminants. Start by filling your mason jar about ¾ of the way with distilled water and put a self-healing injection port lid on it. Put your shot glass and inoculation loop in another jar and cover the tops of your jars with aluminum foil.

Get the pressure cooker ready by placing a canning rack into it or lining the bottom with the rings from jar lids to prevent the jars from touching the bottom. Load the two jars into the pressure cooker and add a couple of inches of water into it. If you're reusing syringes that can be pressure cooked, load them into the pressure cooker as well.

Seal the lid of the pressure cooker and put it onto the stove at high heat until it reaches 15 PSI. Lower the heat so that it maintains 15 PSI and cook everything for 45 minutes. After the time's up, remove the pressure cooker from the heat and allow everything to cool for several hours.

Step Two — Prepare Work Area and Load Glove Box:

While you wait for everything to cool, you can get the work area ready. Start by cleaning the area and wiping all surfaces down with the bleach solution or Lysol. Wipe the interior and the lid of the glove box with the bleach solution or Lysol as well.

After the pressure cooker has fully cooled, put on gloves and rub them down with alcohol. Open the pressure cooker and quickly load the two jars containing your water and equipment directly into the glove box to minimize air exposure as much as possible. Using alcohol, wipe down the packaged sterile syringes, needles, and the bag containing the spore print. Load them into the glove box. Wear clean gloves whenever loading anything into the glove box.

Step Three — Make Syringe:

Put on gloves and rub them down with alcohol. Reach into the glove box and open the first syringe. Put the needle onto the syringe, keeping the plastic protective cover over it. Wipe the injection port on the bottle containing the water down with an alcohol-soaked napkin. Remove the plastic cover from the needle, push it into the injection port, and tilt the jar to fill the syringe with sterile water. Wipe the needle down with an alcohol wipe and replace the protective cover.

Set the shot glass or small jar right-side up in the glove box. Open the plastic bag containing the spore print and unfold it, giving you access to the spores. Using the inoculation loop, scrape a small amount of spores into the glass. Each syringe doesn't require many spores, and a small corner of the print should suffice.

Finally, take the syringe of sterile water and quickly squirt all of the water into the shot glass and suck it back up with the spores now suspended in the water. You can repeat this process for as many syringes as you plan to make. Store the syringes in a cool dry place or the refrigerator for long-term storage. The spore syringes should remain viable for at least a couple of years.

Drying Fruits

Fresh mushrooms tend to not last very long. While it's possible to freeze mushrooms, this often ruins their texture, and, with some species, will make them rather mushy. So if you don't plan to eat your mushrooms within the first week, drying them is one of the best methods for long term storage.

Dried mushrooms can be eaten as is, or reconstituted with water by adding them your soup or another brothy dish. Dried mushrooms can last for years when stored properly. The best way to store dried fruits is in an airtight mason jar with a desiccant pack either in the freezer or in a cool, dry environment.

There are several ways to dry the mushrooms. If you live in a dry environment, such as the desert, you can just use a fan or even the sun to dry the fruits. It's also possible to use an oven on low heat or a desiccant chamber to dry mushrooms. However, the preferred method that requires the least amount of effort is to use a food dehydrator. Food dehydrators are cheap and widely available online or at big box stores such as Walmart.

Drying Mushrooms with the Oven

Necessary Materials:

- Fresh mushrooms

Necessary Tools:

- Oven
- Baking sheet

Step One — Prepare Mushrooms and Oven:

Begin by preheating the oven to 170° Fahrenheit. While you wait for the oven to heat up, wash the mushrooms thoroughly and slice them lengthways. You don't have to be too precise with the thickness of the mushroom slices, so cut them as thick or as thin as you prefer. Layer the mushrooms in a single layer on the baking sheet.

Step Two — Bake the Mushrooms

Place the baking sheet of mushrooms in the oven. Bake them at 170° Fahrenheit for one hour. After an hour, remove the baking sheet and flip the mushrooms. Place them back into the oven and bake for one more hour. Check the mushrooms once the second hour has passed to make sure they're completely dry. You'll know they're dry when they easily break similar to a cracker or, as home cultivators call it "cracker dry."

Step Three — Storage

Put the mushrooms in an airtight container such as a mason jar or zip lock bag with the air removed. A vacuum sealer can also be used for long-term storage. Placing a desiccant pack into the container will help them to stay dry and retain freshness. Store them in a cool, dry place or a freezer for longer term storing.

Drying Using a Food Dehydrator

Necessary Materials:

- Fresh mushrooms

Necessary Tools:

- Food dehydrator

Step One — Prepare the Mushrooms for Dehydration:

Begin by washing the fresh mushrooms thoroughly. Make sure there isn't any substrate left sticking to them as this could be unpleasant to eat. Slice the mushrooms lengthways for quicker dehydration.

It's possible to dehydrate full fruits as well, however, this will take longer. When slicing the mushrooms, keep in mind that thicker slices will take longer to dehydrate than thinner ones.

Step Two — Load the Food Dehydrator:

The food dehydrator usually will have around five to six trays for laying out the food. Place the mushrooms, either sliced or full, in a single layer on each tray. Lay the mushrooms close together to maximize space but make sure they do not overlap, as this will cause the overlapped areas to take longer to dry. As they dry, the mushrooms will shrink creating more space between them.

Step Three — Dehydrate Mushrooms:

Place the mushroom loaded trays back onto the dehydrator. Cheaper food dehydrators often have one temperature setting; if this is your case, you can just turn on the mechanism. If the food dehydrator has an adjustable thermostat, set it to around 110° to 120° Fahrenheit.

The mushroom drying time depends on whether you sliced them or not, and if sliced, the size of the slices. Full-sized fruits can take anywhere from 12 to 24 hours to become fully dry, depending on their size. If you sliced the mushrooms at about ¼", expect them to be dry in around six to eight hours. For slices thicker than ¼", anywhere from 10 to 12 hours should be enough.

The mushrooms are ready once they're "cracker dry," meaning they easily snap in two similar to a saltine cracker or a dry twig. If they have somewhat of a rubbery texture when you attempt to break them, keep them in the dehydrator for more time until they easily break when bent.

Step Four — Storing the Dried Mushrooms:

You have a few options when it comes to long-term storage of the dried fruits. One of the more common methods is to load them tightly into a mason jar with a small desiccant pack. Put as many mushrooms as you can squeeze into the jar as this will minimize their air exposure when stored. The jar can be kept in a cool dry space or your freezer for longer term storage.

You can also store them in a Ziplock freezer bag. Make sure to remove as much air as possible before sealing the bag. This bag can also be kept in the freezer for the longest shelf life. One of the best ways to store the dried fruits is using a vacuum sealer and including a desiccant pack. When stored this way, it's possible to keep them in a freezer for years.

Rehydrating Mushrooms

Dried mushrooms can be rehydrated using a few different methods. The first, and the simplest way, is to add them to a soup or stew. Cooking them in the broth of the soup will allow them to quickly absorb water and bring back their original texture.

It's also possible to put the mushrooms in a bowl and cover them with boiling water. After about 20 to 30 minutes, strain out the water and the mushrooms will be ready to eat. The strained water will also retain the delicious, mushroom flavor, making it great for broths, dressings, and sauces.

Chapter Seven: Popular Mushrooms to Grow

Lion's Mane

Lion's mane is a truly unique species of mushroom. This beautiful mushroom has almost a hair-like appearance when it grows (hence the name lion's mane) and can reach sizes of 4" to 10" as the fruits mature. They are a common saprophytic mushroom that can be found within the Northern United States and Canada. In the wild, lion's mane's favorite food is decaying trees.

This mushroom produces soft, slender spines that give them their 'mane' like appearance. These spines are where a lion's mane mushroom releases its spores from. A young mushroom's spines begin with a bright white color, and they become a pale yellowish-brown color as they mature.

Lion's mane mushrooms are absolutely delicious. They have a tender and somewhat chewy consistency, with a slightly sweet, mild flavor. Many people say that they have a taste reminiscent to scallops, crab, or lobster, making them an excellent ingredient for a variety of vegan seafood dishes. Some popular dishes that use lion's mane mushrooms include mushroom crab cakes, sautéed lion's mane with garlic, and vegan seafood enchiladas.

Health Benefits and Medicinal Properties

Lion's mane mushrooms have a number of nutritional and purported health benefits. Some of the more notable benefits to this species include:

Brain Cell Growth: According to numerous studies, lion's mane mushrooms contain two unique compounds that have neuro-regenerative properties, hericenones and erinacines. These two chemicals may help you from developing symptoms of dementia and Alzheimer's disease as you age.

This has been shown in a few animal studies. In one such study, lion's mane extracts and fruits were given to mice. With the help of this amazing mushroom, the rodents displayed reduced symptoms of memory loss.

In another study, involving humans this time, 3 grams of powdered lion's mane was given to older adults with low-level cognitive impairment over a four-month period. The participants showed significantly improved mental functioning during this time. However, these benefits disappeared once the mushrooms had stopped being administered.

Depression and Anxiety: According to research, lion's mane mushrooms have anti-inflammatory properties that were shown to help relieve symptoms of anxiety and depression. They have also been linked to regeneration of the brain's hippocampus, an area that's associated with emotional response.

Weight Loss and Heart Disease Reduction: In several studies on rats and mice, lion's mane mushrooms were shown to lower triglyceride levels and improve fat metabolism. In one such study, a rat that was fed a high fat diet saw a 27% reduction in triglyceride levels and gained 42% less weight when given lion's mane extract over a 28-day span. Since obesity and a high-level of triglycerides are two predominant causes of heart disease, this is significant.

Stomach Ulcer Protection: While many people associate ulcers with things like too much stress, an abundance of stomach acid, or even spicy foods, these sources are no more than a myth. Most ulcers, including those found in the stomach, are caused by a bacterium. H. pylori. In 1984, Barry Marshall actually drank some of the bacteria to prove that H. pylori the predominant cause of this painful condition.

According to studies, lion's mane mushrooms just so happen to be excellent at preventing the growth of H. pylori. However, this study has only proven that the mushroom can combat this bacterium in a test tube, and hasn't been tested on human stomachs at this time.

High in Antioxidants: According to a study conducted in 2012 on the medicinal properties of 14 different types of mushrooms, lion's mane had the fourth highest level of antioxidants.

A diet rich in antioxidants has many potential health benefits. This includes reduced probability of developing cancer, heart disease, and several other diseases. They can also help fight inflammation and boost your immune system.

Growing Lion's Mane

Below, we'll cover the basics of what you need to know to grow lion's mane mushrooms. Depending on the technique you use, the substrate you use can vary. For example, if you decide to follow the easier PF Tek method to grow lion's mane, you'll use brown rice flour and vermiculite. The other methods will use wood and will produce far more fruit.

Natural Habitat: Lion's mane mushrooms usually grow on old and decaying hardwoods throughout North America. They usually fruit during the fall months.

Difficulty to Grow: This depends on the technique you use, but they range from very easy to grow to fairly difficult.

Ideal Spawn: Lion's mane spawn does particularly well on a variety of grains. Rye grain is especially good for this species. When growing lion's mane spawn, its mycelium will look thin and wispy so it may be hard to tell when it's fully colonized. Shake lion's mane spawn jars or bags often to ensure full colonization

Ideal Substrates: Add the spawn to hardwood sawdust which is ideal for this species. Supplement the sawdust with 10% to 20% wheat bran.

Possible Growing Techniques: PF Tek (easy), grain to sawdust (medium), log grow (fairly difficult).

Where to Grow: Both outdoor (depending on climate) and indoor grows are possible

Fruiting Chamber: The fruiting chamber you use will depend on the technique you choose. For an easy PF Tek grow, the shotgun fruiting chamber is ideal. If spawning from grain to sawdust, use a grow bag. Log grows will be done outdoors but climate must be suitable.

Harvesting: Cut the fruits off as close to the base as possible using a sharp knife. Be careful, and try your best not to damage its spines. Store fruits in the fridge.

Oyster Mushrooms

Oyster mushrooms are an incredibly popular species both commercially and for home cultivation. There are a wide variety of oyster mushrooms you can cultivate, including king oyster, pearl oyster, blue oyster, phoenix oyster, pink oyster, and golden oyster. These mushrooms can vary greatly in size, ranging anywhere from small 2" fruits all the way to large 10" fruits.

These saprotrophic fungi can be found in many subtropical and temperate forests across the globe growing on a variety of decomposing logs. The mycelia of the oyster mushroom is one of the few carnivorous mushroom fungi in the world. It is capable of killing and digesting nematodes (roundworms) and bacteria as a way of obtaining nitrogen.

Different types of oyster mushrooms can come in a variety of colors, ranging from yellow, tan, and pink, to dark gray and brown. Their caps are broad and fan-like with curled edges that will become wavy and lobed upon maturity. Their gills are white and can be found underneath the cap.

The flesh of the oyster mushroom is firm, meaty, and white. They have a bittersweet aroma that some compare to anise, and a texture that's soft and slightly chewy. Their flavor is pretty mild and has a nutty aspect to it. Like lion's mane, some people compare the flavor of oyster mushrooms to seafood. Some common oyster mushroom recipes include pan-fried oyster mushrooms with green onion and garlic, vegan calamari, oyster mushroom po' boys, and mushroom pulled pork.

Health Benefits and Medicinal Properties

There are quite a few benefits to consuming this amazing fungi. Some of these benefits include:

Contains Lots of Key Nutrients: Oyster mushrooms are not only loaded with flavor, but they also have loads of important nutrients. The species contains around 8% of the recommended daily intake of potassium, B vitamins (B1, B3, B5, B6, B12), riboflavin, magnesium, amino acids, pantothenic acid, folic acid, and vitamin C.

Additionally, oyster mushrooms are high in protein, fiber, iron, zinc, phosphorus, calcium, selenium, niacin, and vitamin D.

Boosts Immune System: Thanks to an abundance of beta-glucans, oyster mushrooms are one of the top foods for helping to prepare your immune system to stave off both short-term and long-term illnesses. They do this by helping to keep your immune system in balance rather than stimulating or repressing it.

Good for Dieting: These mushrooms are good for anyone who's looking for something tasty but, at the same time, trying to watch their calorie intake. Oyster mushrooms are low in calories, contain no fat or cholesterol, are gluten free, and have very low sodium.

They make a great cholesterol-free meat replacement in plenty of dishes without having to sacrifice flavor. Some of the great tasting meatless oyster mushroom recipes you can try when trying to shed a few pounds include pulled mushroom tacos, vegan fish, mushroom steaks, vegan carnitas, and fried 'chicken' with oyster mushrooms.

Anti-Inflammatory: Due to the high levels of both beta-glucans and antioxidants that are found in oyster mushrooms, they're a great tool for fighting inflammation. They also contain the unique amino acid ergothioneine, which, according to some studies, also helps to lower inflammation.

Ergothioneine is said to help lower systemic inflammation across your entire body. According to some research, systemic inflammation may contribute to conditions such as diabetes and dementia.

Prevent Plaque Buildup: The ergothioneine that is found in oyster mushrooms can also help to prevent heart disease by reducing the amount of plaque that builds up in your cardiovascular system. The mushrooms have also been shown to help lower cholesterol levels, which can also help in the fight against heart disease.

High in Antioxidants: Antioxidants have loads of health benefits due to their ability to eliminate free radicals in your system. This helps to reduce the damage that oxidation could have on your body. Some of the benefits of a diet high in antioxidants include reduced risk of cancer and lowered chances of heart disease, as well as stopping the vision degeneration that can come with age.

Growing Oyster Mushrooms

There are several different types of oyster mushrooms, and the requirements for growing them (such as fruiting temperature and spawn/substrate requirements) could vary. But the following information is suitable for most varieties.

Natural Habitat: Found in subtropical and temperate forests in much of the world (with the exception of the Pacific Northwest).

They feed on decomposing trees, primarily beech trees, aspen trees, and deciduous trees.

Difficulty to Grow: Easy

Ideal Spawn: There are a variety of options for making your spawn, including sawdust, grains (like millet), and seeds (like wild bird seed).

Ideal Substrates: Again, oyster mushrooms can grow on a wide variety of substrates. Straw is commonly used, as is cardboard, sawdust pellets, and coffee grounds.

Possible Growing Techniques: PF Tek (easy), spawn to substrate (easy), log grow (medium to difficult), five-gallon bucket (easy to medium).

Where to Grow: You can grow oyster mushrooms both outdoor (depending on climate) and indoor.

Fruiting Chamber: Most fruiting chambers can be used to grow oyster mushrooms, but it all depends on the growing technique you use. Shotgun fruiting chamber is best for PF Tek, a grow bag or a 5-gallon bucket are ideal for spawn to substrate grows.

Harvesting: When the caps of your oyster mushrooms begin to turn upwards or flatten out, it's a good time to harvest. If you wait too long, the mushrooms will begin to drop their spores which isn't desirable. To harvest, grab each mushroom at the base and gently twist it. Alternatively, you could use a sharp knife to cut it as low to the base as possible. Dry or store in fridge if you plan to use the mushrooms relatively soon.

Enokitake

Enokitake mushrooms can have a variety of appearances depending on how and where they are grown. The average, pure white, long, and thin enokitake that you'll see in the grocery store appears this way because it is grown in a CO_2 rich environment, which causes it to stretch, and without light, which makes it white. If you grow enokitake mushrooms with light exposure, they'll develop a golden-brown color.

Enokitake mushrooms that grow in the wild look quite different from the cultivated varieties. Wild enokitake are saprotrophic, and generally grow on tree stumps. They are dark brown in color and have a short, thick stem.

If you decide to cultivate this species, you'll either end up with golden enokitake (exposed to light) or white enokitake (no light). You should grow them in a CO_2 rich environment to get the characteristic, small capped, long, thin looking fruits in a tightly packed bouquet.

These mushrooms are tender and crisp in texture and have a crunchy bite to them. Their flavor is relatively mild, peppery, and fruity. Enokitake mushrooms are incredibly common in a lot of East Asian cuisine, but especially in Japanese food. Some common recipes include Korean enoki pancakes, enoki with garlic scallion and soy sauce, nametake, and enoki beef rolls.

Health Benefits and Medicinal Properties

Enokitake mushrooms aren't only tasty and adorable, they're also really good for you. Some of the benefits to consuming this mushroom include:

Very Nutritious: In 100 grams of enokitake mushrooms, you'll get 346 calories. Of those calories, 53% are carbohydrates, 26% are proteins, another 26% are fiber, and only 3% are fats. They contain no cholesterol and are loaded with antioxidants.

Some of the vitamins and minerals found in this healthy mushroom include niacin, iron, thiamin, manganese, copper, selenium, zinc, magnesium, potassium, riboflavin, vitamin D, folate, pantothenic acid, pyridoxine, and calcium.

Possible Cancer Fighting Properties: These mushrooms are currently being studied as a potential way to fight cancer. A scientist in Japan noticed that the residents of Nagano, Japan, had far fewer cases of cancer than those living in other Japanese provinces. One thing that made Nagano different from other provinces is the fact that it's the center of enoki cultivation and an area where the mushroom is widely consumed.

This initial correlation has led to quite a few studies being conducted centering on the relation between enoki mushrooms and cancer. One such study, conducted in 2009, gave rats who were infected with HPV an enoki extract. The rats given the extract were 60% less likely to develop tumors than the rodents who didn't receive an extract. This promising mushroom is still being studied as a possible tool in the fight against cancer!

Good for the Heart: According to animal studies, eating enoki mushrooms could be beneficial for the heart. Not only are they low in cholesterol and loaded with nutrition, but they may actually help to lower your current LDL cholesterol and triglyceride levels.

In a study using hamsters, the animals that consumed enoki extracts had lower levels of both total cholesterol and triglycerides. Their level of LDL, or bad, cholesterol was especially impacted. All of these things together mean better heart health and lower chances of developing cardiovascular problems in the future.

Immunity Boosters: Enoki mushrooms have been used in traditional Chinese medicine to help fight inflammation and boost immunity for some time. Now, there are some studies that may help to back these claims.

According to current research out of Taiwan, these mushrooms contain a special protein that could help to increase your immunity. In this study, mice that were given an enoki extract showed an increase in immune function and were even less likely to develop tumors.

Growing Enokitake

There are multiple ways to grow enokitake and each could yield rather different results. The most standard way is done in a high CO_2 environment, such as a bottle, and in low light conditions.

Natural Habitat: Stumps of Chinese hackberry trees and dead conifer trees. Variations of this mushroom can be found around the world

Difficulty to Grow: Moderately difficult

Ideal Spawn: Enoki mushroom spawn is usually grown on aged hardwood sawdust or paper products. It is also possible to use certain types of grain or seeds.

Ideal Substrates: The best substrate to use is aged hardwood sawdust but straw, wood chips, or even compost could work as well.

Possible Growing Techniques: To achieve the classic elongated, white enokitake, grow in a concealed environment where the mushroom receives lots of CO_2, and give it very little light. For golden brown enoki, expose the mushrooms to more light during the growing process.

Where to Grow: These mushrooms should be grown in an enclosed, high CO_2 containing fruiting chamber indoors (outdoors is possible, but the container still needs to remain enclosed). Enoki mushrooms need a cooler environment to fruit (40° to 60° Fahrenheit), so fruiting in the fridge or a cool basement is a good idea.

Fruiting Chamber: Enokitake mushrooms do well in a high CO_2 environment. Therefore, monotubs and grow bags work well. However, it's even possible to grow this species in a jar or plastic bottle.

Harvesting: Enoki clusters can be pulled and stored in the fridge, and individual mushrooms can be pulled from the cluster and used as needed.

Reishi

The reishi mushroom, unlike most of the others on this list, is more of a medicinal species than an edible species. This mushroom lacks gills, so it releases its spores from small pores located under its caps, making it somewhat unique. The mushroom has a reddish-brown varnished looking cap that grows into a kidney shaped, fan-like appearance. The pores on the underside of its cap will change colors as it ages, transforming from a white color to a mature brown tint.

Different varieties of the reishi mushroom can be found in both Asia and the United States. Reishi are both parasitic and saprotrophic, and can be found growing on trees that are living and dead.

The flesh of a reishi mushroom is soft and corklike, and is normally consumed for its health benefits and medicinal properties. These mushrooms have been used as medicine across much of Eastern Asia for hundreds to thousands of years. They have been used for a wide variety of purposes, such as to fight infection, stave off cancer, and to treat pulmonary diseases.

There are historical records of reishi mushrooms being used in China dating all the way back to 104 BCE. Early medicinal claims stated that these mushrooms were "drugs of immortality" and they were highly revered for their unique properties. They were thought to possess beneficial medicinal and spiritual properties when consumed. According to modern science, there truly are some proven health benefits to consuming this fungi.

Health Benefits and Medicinal Properties

Used as a medicine for thousands of years, there are a lot of potential benefits to consuming this unique fungus:

Strengthens the Immune System: One of the more notable effects of consuming the reishi mushroom and its extracts is what it does to the immune system. This health benefit has been backed by numerous studies. These studies have even shown that compounds found in reishi mushrooms could potentially affect genes within your white blood cells, even altering inflammation pathways in these cells.

Most of the immune system boosting activities of reishi mushrooms have been used on those who are already ill, although there is evidence that they can help healthy people as well. In one study, athletes who had been exposed to stressful conditions saw an increase in their lymphocyte function when given reishi extracts. Most immune system responses to reishi extracts are associated with improvements in white blood cell counts and actions.

Fights Cancer: There have also been numerous studies that have correlated the consumption of reishi mushrooms with fighting or surviving cancer. In one correlation study, 4,000 breast cancer survivors were asked if they had consumed reishi mushrooms.

Over half, 59%, answered yes to this question. While this isn't proof, it does point to a strong correlation.

In another study, reishi mushrooms eliminated cancer cells in a test tube. Again, this may not equate to an ability to kill the cells within a living organism, but it couldn't hurt either.

This mushroom has another benefit for cancer patients: it increases white blood cell activity. Increased white blood cell activity not only improves a patient's ability to fight off the disease, but it can also lead to a better quality of life for them.

Better Quality of Life: The consumption of reishi mushrooms and their extracts has also been shown to decrease both fatigue and depression. In one study, reishi were given to 132 patients suffering from neurasthenia (a disease associated with headaches, fatigue, irritability, and aches). The researchers saw a decrease in fatigue and an improved quality of life after 8-weeks of receiving a reishi extract.

In another study, a reishi extract was given to 48 breast cancer survivors. In only four weeks, the survivors reported that they had less fatigue and experienced a general improvement in their overall wellness. They also reported less depression and anxiety over the course of the study.

Decreased Blood Sugar: According to several studies, reishi mushrooms have been shown to decrease the levels of blood sugar in animals. There is also some evidence that this effect is also present in the humans who consume these mushrooms. However, it is important to note that there have been some mixed results in blood sugar studies regarding reishi mushrooms, so more research is definitely needed.

Better Heart Health: While there are conflicting studies regarding the use of reishi mushrooms and better heart health, there is some promising evidence. In one study where a reishi extract was given to 26 people over a 12-week period, the participants saw an increase in 'good' cholesterol (HDL) and lower triglycerides levels over this time. However, these results have been difficult to replicate in subsequent studies.

Growing Reishi

Reishi are an interesting species to grow and provide some unique formations as they fruit. These mushrooms can be grown several different ways, including both indoors and outdoors.

Natural Habitat: Found both in North America and Asia growing mostly on the stumps of deciduous trees. They are especially fond of maple wood.

Difficulty to Grow: Moderate difficulty.

Ideal Spawn: The best food source to use for reishi mushroom spawn is sawdust.

Ideal Substrates: For growing reishi, either sawdust, hardwood wood chips, or a hardwood log is best. Combining this with bran and gypsum can also be beneficial.

Possible Growing Techniques: PF Tek is possible but not ideal (easy), spawn to substrate (moderate difficulty), log grow (difficult), five-gallon bucket grow (moderate to difficult).

Where to Grow: You can grow oyster mushrooms both outdoor (depending on climate) and indoor.

Fruiting Chamber: Shotgun fruiting chamber (PF Tek), grow bag (spawn to substrate), monotub (spawn to substrate), and five gallon bucket (spawn to substrate).

Harvesting: Once mature, cut or twist and pull your fruits from the base. Dry for long-term storage or put in the fridge if you plan to use them within a short period of time.

Wine Cap

These medium to large sized mushrooms have two to five inch caps and thick, long stems. The caps are a reddish burgundy color when they are young, hence the name wine cap mushrooms. When they mature, the cap becomes a yellowish-brown color and begins to dry. For best flavor, growers tend to pick them while they're still relatively young. Wine cap mushrooms are best grown outdoors and can even be grown alongside your vegetable garden.

These mushrooms are in the agaric family of stropharia, and are one of the few members of this genus which can be eaten. These mushrooms are saprophytic and can usually be found growing on decomposing wood, such as wood chips. They are also known as king stropharia, strophs, godzilla mushroom, and garden giants. Full grown, these mushrooms can get huge with some weighing up to five pounds in total!

Wine cap mushrooms are ideal to eat when they're still young and the caps are still a burgundy hue. The stem of these mushrooms features a nice, firm white flesh and are usually eaten cooked. The texture of wine cap mushrooms tends to be crisp. They taste nutty, earthy, and mild. Some say they have a hint of both potatoes and red wine. Some common recipes using these mushrooms include mushroom caps cooked in embers, mushroom burgers, and oven roasted mushrooms.

Health Benefits and Medicinal Properties

Wine cap mushrooms don't quite have the same level of medicinal benefits of reishi or lion's mane, but they're not without their perks either. Some of the reasons these mushrooms are good for your health include:

Low-Calorie Meat Replacement: With a nice potato-like flavor and a firm texture, these mushrooms are great in all kinds of vegan recipes where they can be used as an ideal meat replacement.

With few calories, no cholesterol, and no fat, they're great if you're trying to watch your weight but don't want to sacrifice flavor. Some delicious recipes that you can make with wine cap mushrooms instead of meat include mushroom filet mignon and mushroom bourguignon.

Potential for Cancer Protection: According to a recent study, a protein isolated from wine cap mushrooms was able to inhibit both liver cancer and leukemia cancer cells. However, this study was conducted in-vitro and the protein has not been tested using either animal or human subjects at this time.

Diabetes: In another study, rats were given diabetes. They were then treated with a compound that was derived from wine cap mushrooms. The rats experienced reduced blood sugar, lower cholesterol, and other improvements.

Growing Wine Cap

While it's not impossible to grow wine caps indoors, your results will likely be disappointing. Therefore, the information below will primarily deal with growing this edible mushroom in an outdoor bed.

Natural Habitat: Wine cap mushrooms can be found growing in wood chips in their native Europe, as well as in North America, Australia, and New Zealand where they have been introduced.

Difficulty to Grow: Moderate

Ideal Spawn: Sawdust is great for making wine cap spawn.

Ideal Substrates: Hardwood chips, straw, sawdust, and compost

Possible Growing Techniques: Spawn to substrate in outdoor garden or mushroom bed.

Where to Grow: Wine cap mushrooms should be cultivated in an outdoor bed.

Fruiting Chamber: Outdoor mushroom bed.

Harvesting: Pinch mushrooms at base and gently twist and pull, or cut with a sharp knife. Store in the fridge if you intend to eat them within a week's time.

Black Poplar

Black poplar mushrooms are also commonly known as velvet pioppini. They grow from small to medium in size, feature fairly long stems, and have caps that range from 1" to 4" in diameter. The color of their caps varies from light brown to dark brown to gray spending on maturity and the area of the cap. They release their spores from the dark gills found under their caps.

These mushrooms can be found growing on stumps and around a wide variety of different trees, including the black poplar tree which lends its name to the mushroom. They are used as a food and have been a part of traditional Chinese medicine.

The texture of these mushrooms has been compared to asparagus, and they are meaty and crunchy. The flavor is slightly sweet, nutty, peppery, and earthy. They are most commonly added to pastas, soups, and stews and are most popular for their great texture. Some delicious recipes featuring black poplar mushrooms include hot velvet pioppini mushrooms with fat raisins in bulghur wheat, beosot muchim, mushroom lover's pasta, and stir-fried mushrooms with garlic and ginger.

Health Benefits and Medicinal Properties

Black poplar or velvet pioppini mushrooms have been a common part of traditional Chinese medicine for quite a while. Some of the more common medicinal uses and health benefits include:

Very Healthy: These mushrooms are loaded with a wide variety of vitamins, minerals, and amino acids. Additionally, they are low in calories and have no fat or cholesterol. Some of the vitamins and minerals you can get from black poplar mushrooms include copper, pantothenic acid, niacin, biotin, folate, vitamin B3, selenium, riboflavin, potassium, and vitamin B2.

Traditional Chinese Medicine: Black poplar mushrooms have been used as a part of traditional Chinese medicine for a variety of purposes. While not proven by current research, some of the traditional uses of this mushroom include: reducing nausea, lowering fevers, and alleviating headaches. They are also purported to have anti-fungal and anti-inflammatory properties.

Growing Black Poplar

Black poplar mushrooms can be grown by following several different techniques and in a variety of different places. Depending on the technique you follow, the difficulty of cultivating this mushroom can vary greatly.

Natural Habitat: Grow in large clusters on deciduous wood logs and stumps. Also found in holes around poplar trees, chestnut trees, tea-oil trees, box elders, cottonwoods, elm trees, willows, and trident maples.

Difficulty to Grow: Easy to Moderate

Ideal Spawn: Spawn is usually grown on sawdust although grain and seeds can be used as well.

Ideal Substrates: The best substrates to use are sawdust, wood chips, grains, or hardwood logs.

Possible Growing Techniques: PF Tek (easy), spawn to substrate (moderate difficulty), log grow (moderate to difficult).

Where to Grow: Can be grown both outdoor and indoor.

Fruiting Chamber: Shotgun fruiting chamber (PF Tek), monotub (spawn to substrate), grow bag (spawn to substrate).

Harvesting: Grab mushrooms by the base and slowly twist and pull to harvest. Additionally, you can use a sharp blade to cut them along the base. Store in the fridge if you plan to use immediately or dry for long-term storage.

Maitake

In the wild, maitake mushrooms can get huge. Normally, the mushroom clusters average from around three to five pounds, but they have been found weighing as much as 100 pounds! The fruiting body of the maitake mushroom has an underground element to it with an inedible leaf-like structure branching out from the base of the above ground mushroom.

Their caps are smooth, wavy, and velvety and vary in color from white, to tan and brown depending on sun exposure. Their spores are released from small pores which are located under the maitake mushroom's cap.

Maitake mushrooms are grown both for their edible and their medicinal properties. They are highly regarded in Japan, and, to this day, the areas where these mushrooms grow wild are protected within the country. In Japan, they are known as the "dancing mushrooms." These saprophytic mushrooms can be found growing around old oak stumps in the Eastern United States, Siberia, and Japan.

These mushrooms have a semi-firm, chewy, and succulent texture once they have been cooked. Their flavor is spicy, somewhat earthy, and with a woody note to it. People usually eat these mushrooms cooked, by either frying, roasting, baking, grilling, or sautéing them. They also make a good addition to salads and soups when consumed fresh. Some popular maitake mushroom recipes include seared maitake mushrooms, grilled Thai marinated maitake mushrooms, maitake wild rice salad, and Kentucky fried maitake.

Health Benefits and Medicinal Properties

Maitake mushrooms have been revered for a number of different health and medicinal properties, especially within Japan. Some of the more notable health benefits to this unique fungi include:

Low in Calories and Nutritious: 100 grams of maitake mushrooms have only 31 calories, almost no fat, about two grams of protein, and nearly three grams of fiber. Additionally, they're loaded with a wide variety of essential vitamins and minerals.

Some of the vitamins found in maitake mushrooms include folates, niacin, pantothenic acid, pyridoxine, riboflavin, thiamin, and vitamin D. The mushroom also contains two essential electrolytes, sodium and potassium. Additionally, they contain the minerals calcium, copper, iron, magnesium, manganese, phosphorus, selenium, and zinc.

Cancer Fighting Properties: According to a fair amount of research, maitake mushrooms are able to protect the body from several common forms of cancer. The primary compound within these amazing mushrooms that is thought to contain the cancer fighting properties is a polysaccharide known as D-Fraction.

D-fraction can enhance certain immune system cells, including white blood cells, cytotoxic T cells, and helper T cells. Together, these immune system cells, with the help of the unique polysaccharide work together to help combat tumor cells.

In one specific study, this compound was given to cancer patients, alone, without additional treatments, and as a result, the growth of metastatic tumor slowed. Additionally, the patients had an increase in natural killer cell growth, the types of cells responsible for killing off tumor cell formations, and a decrease in tumor lab markers. Other studies have shown that D-fraction can help to initiate apoptosis in the cells of human breast cancer patients and bladder cancer patients.

Combat Oxidation: Maitake mushrooms are also very high in antioxidants. This aspect of the fungi allows it to help prevent several serious conditions because it can limit free radicals in the system and combat cell oxidation. Some of the more common conditions that arise from unchecked oxidation include Alzheimer's disease, diabetes, and atherosclerosis.

A simple hot water extraction of maitake mushrooms is enough to create an antioxidant rich solution that has powerful anti-angiogenic activity. Angiogenesis can lead to tumor cell progression, causing a benign growth to become malignant.

These medicinal mushrooms can also help to combat a couple of unique free radicals: the superoxide radical and the hydroxyl radical. These two free radicals are thought to play an important role in the development of several potentially deadly conditions, including myocardial infarction, hypertension, and cardiovascular disease. Some of the antioxidants found in maitake mushrooms include alpha-tocopherol, ascorbic acid, phenols, and flavonoids.

Strengthen the Immune System: Another benefit of consuming maitake mushrooms is an increased immune system response. The polysaccharides contained in this mushroom help increase macrophage, T cell, natural killer cell, and B cell activity, all key components to fighting off diseases.

These mushrooms also have a powerful Immunomodulation effect. This means they help to stabilize, enhance, or depress the immune system depending on the circumstances. This can help your body to regulate an autoimmune disease, fight off a bacterial infection, and recover from a viral infection. The main components of maitake mushrooms responsible for their immunomodulatory effects are beta-glucans.

Protect Against Diabetes: According to several studies, extracts from these wonderful fungi have even been shown to help protect against diabetes. This includes the extract's ability to inhibit the alpha-glucosidase enzyme.

This enzyme is used by the body to break down sugars and starches into glucose, and by inhibiting the enzyme, maitake extracts can slow down the body's rate of glucose absorption. So, just like many anti-diabetic medications, maitake extracts can work as alpha-glucosidase inhibitors.

Growing Maitake

Maitakes are one of the more difficult mushrooms to grow. A large reason for this is the mycelium's unique need for cooler temperatures to fruit (50° to 65° Fahrenheit). Nonetheless, given the right conditions, growing maitake mushrooms at home is totally possible.

Natural Habitat: Found in temperate forests in Japan, the Eastern United States, and Siberia usually growing on the old and decaying stumps of oak trees. They usually fruit in the late summer and early autumn months.

Difficulty to Grow: Moderate to Difficult

Ideal Spawn: The most common spawn material to use is sawdust, although grain can also be used.

Ideal Substrates: Hardwood logs and sawdust or wood chips supplemented with bran.

Possible Growing Techniques: Spawn to substrate (moderate difficulty), log grow (difficult).

Where to Grow: Maitake mushrooms can be cultivated both indoors and outdoors.

Fruiting Chamber: Grow bags and log grows are ideal.

Harvesting: Use a sharp knife to cut the mushrooms off at the base. Store them in the fridge for the short term, or freeze them for long-term storage.

Shiitake

Shiitake mushrooms are the second most commonly consumed mushroom across the globe. You can easily find this tasty fungus in your grocery store's produce aisle, but growing it is so much more entertaining than simply picking some up at the market.

Shiitake are a small to medium sized mushroom, with caps that average anywhere from 4" to 8" in diameter.

These saprophytic mushrooms are commonly found growing in clusters along dead hardwood trees. They are native to East Asia and are predominantly found wild in both China and Japan. In Japan, there are two main types of wild shiitake mushrooms, one of which is mostly used for medicinal purposes and the other as a food source. Shiitake mushrooms are rarely foraged for nowadays due to the fairly easy process of mass cultivation.

The flesh found inside the shiitake cap is cream colored and has a texture that is both spongy and chewy. The stem is usually ivory to light brown in color and has a tough and fibrous texture when eaten. Shiitake mushrooms are usually eaten cooked, and give off a pleasant garlic pine aroma. They tend to have a savory, smoky, earthy, and umami flavor.

These mushrooms can be cooked in a number of different ways. The most popular ways to prepare shiitake mushrooms include frying, baking, sautéing, steaming, boiling, and grilling. They are a common addition to a wide variety of soups, omelets, stir fries, pastas, and vegan cuisine. Some of the more popular shiitake recipes include caramelized shiitake mushroom risotto, broccoli and shiitake mushroom soba noodles, sticky shiitake mushrooms, and sesame asparagus and shiitake mushrooms.

Health Benefits and Medicinal Properties

While most people have tried shiitake as a delicious food source, most people don't know just how amazing these fungi truly are. Not only are they an excellent addition to your stir fry or miso soup, but they also have some surprising health benefits. Some of these include:

Better Heart Health: Due to an abundance of compounds known as sterols, shiitake mushrooms can help to regulate how your liver produces cholesterol. They can also prevent the accumulation of plaque within your cardiovascular system. They prevent plaque buildup by using phytonutrients which can stop the accumulation of cells on the walls of your blood vessels.

Researchers in Japan gave a group of hypertensive rats, shiitake mushrooms as a part of a study. The rats' blood pressure was lowered as a result of eating the fungi. Additionally, after consuming the shiitake mushrooms, the rats in the study saw a decrease in HDL cholesterol.

Reduces Fat: Shiitake mushrooms contain two unique chemicals, eritadenine and b-glucan, both of which have been shown to have fat-reducing properties. One of these chemicals, b-glucan, can decrease appetite, increase satiety, and lower the levels of fat found in the plasma of blood.

In a study on obesity using rats and shiitake mushrooms, shiitakes were given to rodents who were exclusively fed a high-fat diet. The rats that were fed the fungi had a lower level of weight gain than the control group. The researchers concluded that the addition of shiitake mushrooms to a high-fat diet could effectively help to curtail weight gain.

Cancer Killer: Research has also shown some promise in the use of shiitake mushrooms as a tool to help combat certain types of cancer cells. The mushrooms also contain a regenerative chemical known as lentinan which could be useful in restoring damaged chromosomes caused by certain cancer treatment strategies.

A study conducted in 2006 revealed that an extract of shiitake mushrooms could even help to fight tumor growth. During the study, scientists extracted the chemical ethyl acetate from fresh shiitake fruits. The chemical was able to affect apoptosis on live tumor cells, inhibiting the growth at a microchemical level.

Antimicrobial: Shiitake mushrooms even have the ability to kill certain microbes, such as those that cause the gum disease gingivitis. A 2011 study that was carried out in London gave participants struggling with gingivitis either the top mouthwash used for fighting the condition, containing chlorhexidine, or a mouthwash containing a shiitake mushroom extract.

The study concluded by proving that both treatments were effective in combating the bacteria and microbes that led to the condition. However, while the chlorhexidine mouthwash killed both beneficial and infectious bacteria within the mouths of participants, the shiitake extract mouthwash only killed the damaging microbes, leaving the beneficial bacteria intact.

Skin Health: Three vitamins that are excellent for better skin health are also found in shiitake mushrooms. Vitamin E, vitamin A, and selenium, all found in shiitake, help to alleviate the symptoms of acne and the deterioration of skin that comes with aging. The mushrooms also contain zinc, which decreases DHT levels and is also beneficial for the health of your skin.

Energy and Cognition: Due to an abundance of B vitamins, shiitake mushrooms can help your body convert food into energy more efficiently. The mushrooms have also been able to help balance out your hormones, which could increase your cognitive functioning, including better focus.

Growing Shiitake

Depending on the method of growing you choose, shiitake mushrooms can range from easy to difficult to grow. However, there are quite a few different ways to cultivate this mushroom, all providing different yields and levels of difficulty, making it a great option for both beginners and advanced growers.

Natural Habitat: Found primarily in warm and moist climates in Southeast and Eastern Asia. They primarily grow in groups on dead and decaying hardwood trees, including oak, chestnut, shii, beech, maple, poplar, sweetgum, chinquapin, ironwood, mulberry, and hornbeam

Difficulty to Grow: Easy to moderate

Ideal Spawn: Shiitake spawn can be grown well on both sawdust and grain.

Ideal Substrates: Hardwood chips, hardwood sawdust, and hardwood logs.

Possible Growing Techniques: PF Tek (easy), spawn to substrate (moderate), log method (difficult).

Where to Grow: Can be grown both indoors and outdoors.

Fruiting Chamber: Shotgun fruiting chamber (PF Tek), grow bag (spawn to substrate), log grow.

Harvesting: Grab the fruit at the base and slowly twist and pull to harvest. Alternatively, you can cut them at the base using a sharp knife. Store them in the fridge if you intend to use them within about a week, otherwise, you can dry or freeze them for long-term storage.

Luminescent Panellus

While not generally an edible or medicinal mushroom, this species is grown purely for decorative purposes. While technically they can be eaten, the bitter taste of luminescent panellus makes them undesirable for this purpose. What makes these mushrooms special is their bioluminescence.

The mushroom grows in dense clusters on the stumps and logs of deciduous trees in many countries across the globe. They develop fan-like kidney shaped caps that are about 1.2 inches broad. These caps vary in color from orange to yellow and brown. The bioluminescence is generally seen around the gills of the mushrooms and along the junction where the stem and cap meet. The mycelium can also exhibit bioluminescence.

This mushroom's visible luminescence is thought to be the result of a single dominant allele. This mushroom has also been considered a candidate for use in bioremediation due to its ability to remove toxins and pollutants from the environment in which it's grown.

Growing Luminescent Panellus

This mushroom isn't the easiest to grow, but its awesome display of lights make it a unique species to cultivate.

Natural Habitat: Found across the globe, including the eastern United States, New Zealand, Australia, Europe, China, and Japan. It's usually found on hardwood trees, logs and stumps including oak, birch, pecan, hickory, maple, and American hornbeam.

Difficulty to Grow: Moderate

Ideal Spawn: Sawdust makes the best food source for spawn, but grain has also been used successfully.

Ideal Substrates: Wood chips, sawdust, grain, and even agar.

Possible Growing Techniques: Spawn to substrate (moderate difficulty), log grow (difficult).

Where to Grow: Indoors or outdoors is possible depending on climate.

Fruiting Chamber: Grow bag (spawn to substrate), log grow.

Chapter Eight: Troubleshooting Common Problems

Contaminations Ruining Grows

If the grows are constantly plagued by contaminants, there could be several reasons for this. But, the number one reason for contaminations is poor sterile technique. Therefore, make sure you're always using a glove box when inoculating your substrate and you're pressure cooking everything for a substantial amount of time. It's also vital that you wear clean gloves when working in a glove box and you rub your gloves down with 70% isopropyl alcohol frequently.

Make sure that you clean your glove box and work area thoroughly before doing any work with it. Using a bleach solution that's 10% bleach and 90% water should be enough, but wiping it all down with 70% isopropyl alcohol couldn't hurt either. Also, wipe anything you're putting into your glove box with alcohol as well. Your syringes could also be contaminated, in which case, you'll need to buy or make new syringes.

The grain you're inoculating could be another issue. Some bacteria are extremely heat resistant when dormant and are able to survive the pressure-cooking process. To kill these pesky bacteria, make sure you're soaking your grain for 24 hours prior to sterilization. This will allow these bacteria time to sprout, at which point it will be more vulnerable to the heat during the sterilization process.

If you're doing all of the above and you're still experiencing lots of mold during the grows, it could be your home or growing environment. Check the growing area for mold growing on the walls or under sinks. Areas with lots of mold will have far more spores floating in the air. This will make it much more difficult to grow, however, with proper sterile technique, it's still possible.

If bacterial contaminations are a common issue for the grows, make sure you're not adding too much water to the substrates. You want the grains or wood substrates to be at field capacity, but not dripping wet. Excess water in the substrate is one of the more common causes of bacterial contaminations. Also, if using grain, make sure you're not cooking them so long that the kernels crack or pop open. This, too, can cause more frequent bacterial contaminations such as wet spots.

Finally, temperature can lead to more frequent contaminations. Using a high heat incubation chamber or warmer environment may cause the mycelium to grow faster, but it also will make a variety of molds grow faster. Mycelium is pretty contaminant resistant once it has matured, but a warm environment may cause a mold to grow quickly and prevent the mycelium from ever reaching maturity. So, room temperature colonization, while slower, is also less prone to contamination.

Substrate Isn't Colonizing

If it seems like you're doing everything right, but nothing seems to be growing, no contaminations, no mycelium, just blank substrate, there could be a few possible issues. First, check the temperature you're colonizing in.

If it is either too hot or too cold, the temperature could be causing the issue. While the ideal temperature is dependent on the species you're growing, trying to colonize in extreme temperatures could be killing your mycelium. Try moving it to a room temperature environment for colonization and see if things improve.

Another potential issue could be a lack of fresh air. While you don't need a lot of fresh air during colonization, mycelium does need to breathe for it to grow. Make sure you're using jars or grow bags that have a hole (covered with a filter of some sort) for fresh air exposure. If using jars, try making and using the self-healing injection port lids discussed in chapter six. These lids offer good fresh air exchange and can be used on any grow that requires mason jars.

The substrate you're using could also be too dry. While a substrate that's too wet is more prone to bacterial contaminations, using a substrate that's too dry could inhibit mycelial growth. Try to always get your substrate to field capacity. This means either soaking it or boiling it longer, depending on the substrate you're using. Determining the correct moisture level of your substrate may take a bit of trial and error, but, with time, it'll become second nature.

Light could also be an issue. Setting a jar in direct sunlight may potentially kill the mycelium. However, you do want some ambient light. While the jars will colonize in complete darkness if absolutely necessary, some ambient light has been shown to lead to faster colonization rates.

Finally, if you're using a spore syringe, you may not be waiting long enough. Each spore syringe contains potentially millions of spores. Each one one of these spores has slightly different genetics than the others. Some of these genetics will offer quick sprouting and growing mycelium, while others tend to grow quite slowly. I've had jars that took over a month before I saw any mycelial growth in them whatsoever. So, if using spores, be patient, or, better yet, switch to a liquid culture or agar.

Small Yields

When the yields are consistently small, there may be a problem, or you might just need to try a different growing technique. If you're doing PF Tek or a bottle/jar grow, you can expect relatively small yields. These techniques, while relatively easy, use a small amount of substrate and won't provide nearly as many fruits as other growing methods, such as monotubs and outdoor beds.

The humidity level of the grow area is another possible issue. If you're growing in an indoor fruiting chamber such as a monotub or shotgun chamber, you should see water droplets form on the sides of your chamber. Spraying your chamber with water using a simple spray bottle a few times a day will help to increase the relative humidity. You can also add a hygrometer to your fruiting chamber to accurately monitor the humidity. For ideal growing conditions, you want a relative humidity level of 80% to 90%,

Mushrooms also need a lot of fresh air to thrive. This is especially true for certain species, such as oyster and maitake. If growing a species that requires a lot of fresh air in an indoor fruiting chamber, such as a monotub, don't expect giant yields. To increase the yields, switch to an outdoor bed or log grow. With an indoor fruiting chamber, installing a small fan to the tank, or putting a fan in the room, will also increase air flow. Fanning your fruiting chamber several times a day using the lid of the tub or a paper fan will also help expel excess CO_2 and introduce fresh air.

The genetics of the mushrooms could also be the cause of a small yield. This is generally a problem when inoculating from a spore syringe or print, or using a liquid culture made from spores. Every spore on the print or in the syringe has different genetic traits, and some of these genetics are more prone to smaller yields. You can fix this by using colonized agar or a liquid culture that was made through cloning high yielding genetics. Liquid cultures or agar plates found on cultivation websites should offer good genetics, or you can make your own.

Colonized but Not Fruiting

For an indoor grow, environmental factors such as light, humidity, and temperature could be responsible for the cake not fruiting. Use a hygrometer to make sure the humidity level is around 80% to 90% in the fruiting chamber. Spraying the sides of the container down with a spray bottle will help to increase the relative humidity within the grow chamber.

It also may be too hot or cold in the fruiting chamber. Most species of mushrooms will grow fine at room temperature. However, extremely cold temperatures will greatly slow the rate of growth while temperatures which are too hot could kill the mycelium altogether. One cause of an overly hot fruiting chamber is the lighting. Make sure to use a light that doesn't produce too much heat and suspend the light at a decent distance away from the mycelium. Compact fluorescent lighting or LED bulbs are ideal as they produce little to no heat.

Speaking of lighting, make sure the indoor fruiting chamber is receiving enough of it. Light helps to initiate pinning, and a proper light cycle is ideal. For the indoor chamber, the ambient light from a window will work, just make sure it's not in direct sunlight. If using artificial lighting, you want to try to imitate a natural light cycle. This means 12 hours of light and 12 hours of darkness. Using a timer for this will simplify the process.

Not enough fresh air could also delay pinning or completely suffocate the mycelium in extreme situations. This isn't an issue for outdoor beds, but if using an indoor fruiting chamber, make sure you've drilled enough holes into it and that the holes are large enough. Certain species do poorly without enough air, so if the species you're growing requires plenty of airflow, you may just want to consider doing an outdoor grow instead.

Regularly fanning the growing chamber using the lid of the container or some other fan several times a day is also important to make sure you're expelling the CO_2 and introducing fresh air regularly. You can also install a small computer fan into the fruiting chamber or put a fan on low setting in the same room to increase airflow.

If the substrate is too dry, this could be another problem. If the substrate looks shriveled and dry, it is possible to soak the cake to add more water to it. If doing PF Tek, simply put the pint-sized cakes in a large bowl, put a plate on them to keep them submerged, and soak for about 24 hours before reintroducing them to the fruiting chamber. For larger cakes, a five-gallon bucket or plastic storage bin can be used to soak them for around the same amount of time.

If the outdoor bed isn't fruiting, it could be for similar reasons, such as humidity, temperature, and lack of moisture. Make sure to keep the outdoor substrate as moist as possible, but not by soaking it. Instead, sprinkle it with a hose regularly. However, if you live in an overly hot and dry environment you may be out of luck and should consider just growing indoors. The season is vital for outdoor beds as well. Depending on where you live, spring, summer, and fall are the most likely times to see fruiting. After a heavy rain when the humidity level is high is when the mushrooms will likely pin.

Dealing With Contaminants

While it may be hard to throw all your hard work in the trash, when you see a contaminant starting to grow, it's often the only option. This is especially true for mold contamination, since by the time you see them, it's usually too late. With some molds, such as cobweb, spraying it with a 3% hydrogen peroxide solution early enough may save your work but don't count on it.

The problem with mold contaminations is that they create spores which will get into the air and increase the likelihood of future contaminations. This is why most mushroom growers will throw away any cake or substrate at the first sign of mold growth. While bacterial contaminations can be a little more forgiving, mold is usually a lost cause.

With a bacterial contamination, the best course of action is to usually toss it as well. However, I have had wet spot contaminated jars where the mycelium overtook the contamination and still fruited with good results. Therefore, this is a judgment call on your part. However, if you see a large wet spot and the mycelium has completely stopped growing, it's best to toss the jar and start over.

Fungal gnats, while gross, aren't a huge deal. They will feed on the mycelium and mushrooms but won't ruin the grow. The larger risk with these pests is that they could potentially introduce other contaminants such as mold. Mites also don't pose a huge problem, with some types actually being beneficial.

For outdoor grows, there are more types of insects and pests that can infiltrate the mushroom garden. Things like worms and other insects, or birds and other animals may feed on your hard work. To minimize this issue, harvest early and often. The longer the mushrooms are outside and exposed to the environment the more likely they are to become something else's food.

www.ingramcontent.com/pod-product-compliance
Lightning Source LLC
Chambersburg PA
CBHW071447070526
44578CB00001B/242